mindful living

mindful living

a guide to the everyday magic
of feng shui

anjie cho & laura morris

CICO BOOKS
LONDON NEW YORK

Published in 2024 by CICO Books
An imprint of Ryland Peters & Small Ltd
20–21 Jockey's Fields   341 E 116th St
London WC1R 4BW   New York, NY 10029

www.rylandpeters.com

10 9 8 7 6 5 4 3 2 1

A CIP catalog record for this book is available
from the Library of Congress and the British
Library.

ISBN: 978-1-80065-346-7

Printed in China

Designer: Geoff Borin
Commissioning editor: Kristine Pidkameny
Senior designer: Emily Breen
Art director: Sally Powell
Creative director: Leslie Harrington
Head of production: Patricia Harrington
Publishing manager: Carmel Edmonds

MIX
Paper from
responsible sources
FSC
www.fsc.org   FSC® C106563

contents

foreword 6

introduction: starting the path 8

chapter 1 discovering magic in your home 12

chapter 2 the feng shui of color 28

chapter 3 the bagua mandala 42

chapter 4 reading your floor plan 66

chapter 5 the everyday magic of plants 86

chapter 6 your monthly qi forecast 94

chapter 7 mindful rituals for the seasons 112

chapter 8 connections to the natural world 124

chapter 9 living well with feng shui 136

resources and further reading 140

index 141

picture credits 143

acknowledgments 144

foreword by Katherine Metz,

writer and archivist of Pure Professor, a collection of the teachings
of His Holiness Grandmaster Professor Lin Yun

Years ago, I found myself at a dinner party seated next to the
conductor of one of the longest running shows on Broadway.
Wanting to make conversation but unable to think of what I might
have in common with a world-renowned conductor, I simply asked
him what it's like to do the same thing night after night. His answer
surprised and delighted me, and I realized that we did indeed
share a curious way of knowing things. Magic.

He told me that, while conducting the evening before, he heard
another sound "slow-dancing" above the notes of his string section.
A sound not part of the show's score, but rather silent, hidden
notes of sadness; sound that was as real and as present to him as
the music the audience was enjoying. Feeling beyond the notes, he
immediately knew that his first violinist had had a very bad day. His
heart met hers in a flash of intuitive insight. Without missing a beat,
the two masterful musicians nodded gently to one another in a
personal moment of appreciation and understanding—touched
by magic—never to be the same again.

I recognized straightaway that such enchantment is familiar
to me. I, too, have experienced moments when, at warp speed, the
familiar and the fathomless become inquisitive friends, beckoning
me to join them sensuously exploring the hidden in the ordinary.
This is magic, and it has an intriguing sense of authority despite the
unyielding chatter of our logical minds. We must not let its power
of connection and kindness be explained away—for it is often
uncannily right and vastly more interesting.

The world is calling for us to extend our curiosity, knowing
that magic awaits us—even if we find ourselves on the edge of
discomfort. With heartfelt intention and timeless wisdom, feng

shui scholars Laura and Anjie are gently and bravely asking us to step outside what is known. To mindfully embrace and find ease in the spaciousness and natural rhythm of a magical moment. To come home to the center of our being.

We all live under the same stars and jeweled moon and have a special responsibility to be creative and kind. As we put our ears down close to our soul and listen along with them, we come to know more about who we are and of what we are capable. Magic is an inherently human capability, and uniquely yours. How will you give magic a reasonable voice in a world in need of beautiful hearts and minds?

introduction: starting the path

walking the labyrinth together

The seed for this book was planted while walking together in a labyrinth. It was a warm April afternoon in 2017, on the banks of the Hudson River in Upstate New York. We were invited by our feng shui mentors to co-teach their certification students during an annual retreat. It was really the first time that either of us had taught an "official" class. It was also the first time we had spent more than a few minutes together. Although we had the same teachers, we studied a few years apart.

During our time exploring the grounds, our slow meandering found us at the mouth of a labyrinth. The typical use of the word "labyrinth" refers to a maze, expressing a feeling of confusion and perhaps chaos. However, a physical labyrinth, in contrast, manifests as a single path. One enters, reaches the center, then exits following the same thread back to the beginning. It's quite clarifying to be guided along one line in a clear and straightforward direction. Such simplicity offers peaceful opportunities for spacious reflection.

This sacred geometric pattern roused something within us that day. We recognized that we shared the same aspirations to contribute to the world through the medium of feng shui. We saw that we both place tremendous value on our lineage of teachers and on teaching with the utmost sincerity. And so the Mindful Design Feng Shui School and our collaborative partnership was born.

In all our work together, our intention is to offer respect to East and West, and to heaven and Earth. We aspire to explore and bridge Eastern and Western perspectives with responsibility. We seek to express egolessness without dogma, by modeling that there isn't one "correct" way, nor a guru on a pedestal who knows everything and has all the "right" answers. We also both wish to see feng shui shared with the transformational aspects of mindfulness and gentleness. This seems to be missing in the mainstream. This is where our name, "Mindful Design," comes from. The universe presented us with a rare opportunity to explore a partnership that continues to be profoundly meaningful and spiritually nourishing.

why we wrote this book

Our intention is to create a unique offering that is helpful, digestible, and of service to the world. Over our five-year business partnership (almost like marriage!), we have delighted in sharing and contrasting our yin and yang: our complementary and balanced personalities, lifestyles, and cultural backgrounds. Anjie is Korean-American, a practicing architect, living in a high-rise apartment in New York City. She's a Buddhist and studies various Asian arts, including the *chanoyu* tea ceremony and *ikebana* flower arranging. Laura is Canadian of Italian descent. A designer and artist, she splits her time between the countryside of Ontario and rural Tuscany. She is also a Tarot card reader and has a keen interest in Italian folk practices. Therefore, our own interests and personal ancestries have cultivated the foundation of this book and the way that we teach.

We encourage our students and readers to appreciate their own local and cultural practices in tandem with the feng shui studies that come from Asia. In our current connected world, it would be a missed opportunity to ignore the richness and diversity at our fingertips. Please don't forget where you come from or your own lineages that make up who you are.

our lineage

We would like to share with our readers a short note about our feng shui lineage. We teach from the BTB (Black Sect Tantric Buddhist) lineage. There are dozens of schools of feng shui, and we consider all of them equally meaningful and valuable, however, we teach directly from the BTB teachings as transmitted to us. We continue to study with and are mentored by our dearest teachers Katherine Metz and Rosalie Prinzivalli. They learned the practice of feng shui directly from our root teacher, his Holiness Grandmaster Lin Yun.

Above We invite you to carve your own path with this book. Pause, feel, and mindfully experience the everyday magic around you.

Above Color and shape offer opportunities to connect more deeply with your home. Red is vibrant and magnetic and the fresh yellow flowers invite health and well-being.

We are also beneficiaries of wisdom traditions that include Taoist, Buddhist, Chinese folk, Tibetan Bön, and Tantric lineages. We are part of a golden chain of wisdom. These feng shui practices are not ours, and we cannot claim them as our own. We are one branch on a great tree that has grown from deep roots.

how to use this book

The following pages are intended as a modern and practical guide for beginners. This book is an introduction to exploring the everyday magic of feng shui. Throughout time, humans have been searching for a deeper connection and meaning with their homes and environments. Common questions naturally arise like: "Why does my house still feel 'off,' even after I spent a week decluttering and organizing?" or "How do I feel more at home in my home?" As you read through this book, we encourage you to explore the array of feng shui tools we offer. We hope to inspire you to continually investigate all the questions that arise in your heart, with the invitation to examine the interconnection between the visible and invisible.

We look forward to connecting with our long-time followers as well as new friends that are longing for more magic in their healing practices and their everyday life, or are simply curious and seek to understand more about their relationship with their home and spaces.

Here are some gentle guidelines for using this book:

1 Like the labyrinth, this book may present the reader with moments of thoughtfulness and reflection. Feel free to pause and to move backward and forward as you wish. We intend for this book to read as like a path in which you can receive and rejoin at your own pace.

2 We include "Everyday Magic Rituals" in different parts of the book. They are recommended, but not required. The idea of a ritual includes the practical and esoteric. We encourage you to focus not only on the doing but also on the reflections and sense perceptions that arise.

3 We believe that in some cases the reader would benefit from additional audio or visual instructions. Keep an eye out for these, as they are peppered throughout the book (see Resources, page 140).

4 Kindly consider all of our teachings as a way to receive insight and awareness. Sometimes things will not resonate and, if that's the case, please let them go. We encourage you to liberate yourself from dogma and allow your energy to flow. Receive what is helpful; release what is not.

5 Finally, this is not a book about fixing your home so that you can have a perfect life. Instead, let the imperfections guide you so they can illuminate your path. We look forward to walking this path alongside you.

Above Like this eclectic collection of flowers and plants, there is room for variety in our feng shui and lives.

discovering magic in your home

- mindfulness in everyday magic
- the "yes/and" paradox
- qi: wind and water
- everyday magic ritual: a room-by-room exploration

mindfulness in everyday magic

Feng shui is a kind of everyday magic and anyone can do it. You don't need special abilities. The magic of feng shui is not about having psychic abilities or superpowers. It is about being in harmony with the world and your surroundings, las well as your connection to self and others. Feng shui offers practices to cultivate your life-force energy, known as qi, so you can become more aware and sensitive to the world around you. It also offers guidance to attune you with the energy of the Earth, nature, and seasonal cycles. Feng shui has frameworks, systems, symbolism, and language that allow all of us to divine and interpret this unseen energy.

Like the everyday magic of many cultures, feng shui is grounded, practical, and simple. It is a life view that connects heaven and Earth, the esoteric and the mundane, with humans standing in the middle. With it you can understand your home, nature, and the tangible world, tapping into something even bigger. These practices offer opportunities to awaken, create awareness, and highlight stuck patterns and perceived limitations. Feng shui allows us to hear what the universe is saying if we can open up and listen.

what is feng shui?

We often define feng shui as the mindfulness practice of paying attention to the details of our spaces. Feng shui presents simple techniques and adjustments to create mindful opportunities for everyday magic. Mindful intention, ritual, and awareness have the potential to transform rushed and thoughtless tasks into magical, healing, and insightful teachings. When you practice feng shui this way, blending the everyday with the metaphysical, the two realms become intertwined. A quiet change in a home can be so much more with the mindful application of feng shui.

When you tap into the invisible and energetic side of your home, you become conscious of much more. Everyday feng shui practices can also become deeply personal and transformative. There is true magic in creating a mindful and intentional friendship with your home. Not many people realize that a huge part of feng shui is becoming attentive to how your space makes you feel. As you move through this book and begin to play with this everyday magic, try to notice how your home feels and how you feel. You may notice you are lighter and happier; maybe you even experience tingles and sensations as you perform an adjustment. Or you might have new glimmers of insight and "a-ha" moments. No matter what you feel (or don't feel) our aspiration is that you will be more connected to your home and environment after exploring the ancient practice of feng shui.

Right A simple flower arrangement can inspire a moment of contemplative reflection.

the "yes/and" paradox

Above Everyday objects in our home offer opportunities to explore the nuances of yin and yang. The black yin color of the coffee contrasts with the white yang color of the cup.

The philosophy of feng shui is both inviting and accessible, while at the same time complex and intricate. Feng shui examines how humans live with and experience the world. The teachings explore the visible parts of your home and environment to reveal the invisible and perhaps hidden aspects within your life. Your living space can be a path toward transformation. Your home is a container for energy. It is also your companion and guide. The feng shui of your home can teach you how to recognize and give shape to this energy. Feng shui challenges us to view the world using both yin and yang, by seeing below the surface and reading the energy through the physical space.

What does it mean to see the world with a "yin and yang" view? Yin and yang are often defined as two opposing forces that combine to create everything in the whole world. Basically, two fundamental types of energy mixing together in varying degrees to create all things everywhere—pretty important stuff.

The physical and tangible realm is considered yang: what you can see and touch. Yin refers to the invisible side of things, that which is below the surface or unseen. While this is true, we also take great care to emphasize the importance of stepping beyond conventional or superficial definitions in feng shui. Instead, the principles of yin and yang skillfully teach us that there is an opportunity to reconsider fixed or narrow points of view.

For example, a cup of freshly brewed espresso may be described as yin because coffee is wet, black, and has steam rising from it. These are all so-called yin qualities. However, there are yang aspects at play here as well: the demitasse cup is hard and white, and the liquid is hot. The cup receives and holds the coffee, which is yin. The coffee fills the empty cup, which is yang. Therefore, this situation is both yin and yang. Yin and yang is an exploration of the non-binary. It's yin. It's yang. It's "yes/and." Both can be true, and something can be yin and yang at the same time.

This "yes/and" paradox gives us more flexibility and space to understand feng shui. Yes, feng shui is about making changes to your home. And yes, it's also a personal journey. It's both at the same time! Feng shui principles can be applied to your home, but also to your life and your mindset. You can implement feng shui changes to your bedroom, whole home, neighborhood, city, and beyond. Feng shui holds within it many layers and nuances.

Let's open up to the wisdom of yin and yang and relax our preconceived notions of what we think is graspable, solid, and unchanging. Instead, "yes/and" teaches us to open, receive, and challenge our rigid expectations that can create fear and stagnation. Just like water, how can we flow, transform, and offer more kindness and acceptance to ourselves and others?

yin and yang qualities

Here's a short list of yin and yang qualities. In reality, this list is positively endless!

yin	yang
moon	sun
feminine	masculine
right brain	left brain
soft	hard
black	white
midnight	noon
empty	full
cool	warm
death	life
small	big
wet	dry
interior	exterior
low	high
quiet	loud

qi: wind and water

Above A colorful and whimsical arrangement of meaningful treasures is one way to lift your qi, and in turn, cheer you up.

Feng shui is an ancient Chinese wisdom tradition that is over 4,000 years old. The words *feng* and *shui* translate to "wind" and "water," two elements that are essential for human life on Earth. Breath and hydration sustain our human bodies as well as the planet. Wind is our breath, and science tells us that we are comprised of over 60 percent water.

Together, wind and water create motion. The great ocean currents stream, flow, and connect the globe, sustaining entire ecosystems. The symbolism of wind and water is at the heart of feng shui. Wind is movement and flow. And in stillness, wind ceases to exist. Similarly, water must flow and move to maintain vitality, to stay clean and useful. Still water becomes stagnant and lifeless. Therefore, the words "feng shui" point to life-giving movement and flow.

Qi is this life-giving source. Qi is life-force energy and is the foundation and everyday magic of feng shui. It is the feeling of vigor walking through a lush, green forest as well as the sense of ease and serenity while sitting on an empty beach watching the sun set. Sometimes qi may show up as a tingling sensation; other times it may be expressed by a bird flying across the sky.

While we believe it is not something easily defined, you can think of qi as vital energy, a life force that flows through everything. Early Taoist texts advise on how a person can improve their good fortune, resilience, longevity, and health. The strength of your life force depends on your qi. Your qi must flow freely within your body as well as throughout your environment, unencumbered and without blocks. Like wind and water, we look toward the movement of qi. Ideally, the feng shui of your home protects and supports the qi. A home's qi is most desirable, healthy, and happy when the energy is flowing, inviting, and active.

exploring the qi of your home

In feng shui we see no separation between the outer environment and one's inner being. Therefore, your home influences you as much as you influence it. Many people don't realize the potential of feng shui as a healing opportunity. As you begin to implement feng shui in your home, you might be surprised that feng shui is also a divination practice. Our physical spaces are symbolic and have deeper meaning. But don't forget the "yes/and" paradox. When you see "bad feng shui" in your home, it may correspond to good news. Perhaps your non-conscious mind has invited that feng shui detail into your home because you're at an opportune time in your life to unpack, explore, and heal that wound.

Divination might sound exclusive or extraordinary, but the way we are using it here is connected to the notion of everyday magic. It's not anything uncommon or exotic. Instead, we encourage you to use divination as a path to become friendly with your most ordinary self. Open yourself up to an opportunity to be vulnerable and see things just as they are. Our homes have so much to say, but we often voluntarily close our ears.

Our conditioning and modern lives tend to sweep us farther and farther away from our phenomenal world. What are the messages that are right in front of you that you miss every single day? We don't need to have unique and special gifts to receive these messages. Divination is acknowledging the divine wisdom that is within you.

As you move through the book, we'll explore how feng shui is a way to receive messages and heal. This includes the better-known feng shui tools, including the use of colors, plants, and the bagua mandala, as well as how to apply feng shui to floor plans. But we will also include lesser-known magical tools such as flower essences, meditation, cartomancy, and simply connecting to our own senses and experience.

Above Take time to appreciate the colors and textures of everyday objects (and experiences) in your life. Delight in the simple details.

a room-by-room exploration

This ritual, in which you explore each room in your home in turn, will introduce you to the symbolic meaning of the different living spaces in your home. In each room, we offer three helpful suggestions to review, but this is not an exhaustive checklist of things to do, and not all are required. We want you to start your path of mindful living with ease! How you begin will set the qi in motion for the steps that follow.

1 If possible, review these recommendations while physically present in the room. Remember, this is an everyday magic ritual so it's not just about doing, but also includes considering and taking note of how you feel. Do you like, dislike, or feel neutral about the space? Notice any thoughts and reflections that may arise. Sometimes the room might not require any adjustments.

2 When moving through this home scan, also notice which room is the most easeful and the quality of the qi present. Which rooms feel most in alignment with you, and which feel challenging? Are there spaces that are neglected and accumulating dust, or ones that are lively and full of joy? Notice and have curiosity, open your eyes, and learn what your home is sharing.

3 If you find that you have a number of items to address, we recommend that you begin with one room and with the most attractive task. Making a simple change can kickstart the qi. In our experience, it's not ideal to start with the most challenging items because you may self-sabotage and give up.

4 After the first task is completed, celebrate! Acknowledge your success. Let a friend know! Then continue and select the next achievable task. And so on. Remember, you can always come back to this list when it calls you.

entry foyer

Your entry and front door area are your face to the world. In feng shui we call this the "mouth of qi" because it's where the energy from the outside has an opportunity to enter your home and your life.

Front door: Make sure that the front door can open a full 90 degrees and that there are no obstacles stopping the door from opening. When your front door can open fully, you are able to receive an abundance of opportunities. When it cannot open fully, only a portion can come in.

Lighting: How is the lighting in the foyer? The ability to clearly see and illuminate the entry foyer affects your visibility and clarity in the world. Lighting both invites and offers clarity.

Doormat: Create an inviting entry with a doormat. This is grounding and becomes a place for the qi to cultivate. Be sure the mat is pleasing to you and complements your home. It should be not too small and not too big. Keep the doormat (and the foyer in general) clean, swept, and tidy.

Above right A bright, sunny, or well-lit entryway illuminates opportunities in your life.

Right The front door is a portal for qi to enter the home. Soft, pale green colors are calming and soothing. An earth-toned rug or doormat made from natural fibers helps to ground and settle the energy.

living room

The living room is exactly what it sounds like—a room for living. It's a place to hang out, and where we invite and greet friends, family, and guests. It is a common area or public space in your home and so we want to create a welcoming room. Many modern homes have moved to a less formal living room situation, like a family room or den, but the same guidelines apply.

Seating: Take care to be generous with the seating. Is there a comfortable spot for each member of the family? In addition, make sure there is room for friends and family, or other visitors.

Focal point: While a TV is completely acceptable, you may decide to create a primary (or even secondary) focal point around something else. A low, central coffee table, for example, can be gathered around and will encourage conversation. What is the qi you aspire to cultivate in a space for living?

Brighten: This is a room that can benefit from an abundance of yang energy. You can facilitate this by adding brighter colors with home accents or including plenty of lighting to illuminate and lift the qi.

dining room

The dining area is where you gather with friends and family to celebrate and enjoy a meal together. In feng shui it represents your friendships and community. In modern homes, the dining table is also multifunctional and can be used for homework, crafts, or as a workspace.

Activate the qi: Many dining tables end up being used for purposes other than dining. This is okay, but we also encourage you to dine there. Host a dinner party! Even if you're dining for one, explore how you can create an inviting experience.

Fresh flowers: Place a vase of freshly cut flowers on your dining room table as often as possible. Even a single bloom can transform the energy.

Seating: As for the living room, make note of the available seating at the dining table. Ideally, keep a few extra chairs to welcome more kindred spirits into your home and life.

Left A thoughtfully arranged dining table invites community. The color white supports conversation, while pink encourages softness and receptivity.

Opposite Books represent knowledge in feng shui. One of the many ways to arrange your favorite books is by color.

discovering magic in your home

kitchen

One of the most used areas of the home, the kitchen is also considered a symbol of health, resources, and nourishment. In this space, fire and water alchemize and transform into medicine for our body and spirit.

Mind your stove: In feng shui, the condition of your stove influences your finances and overall well-being. Therefore, the stove should be kept clean and in working order.

Tidy your food storage: Regularly review your cupboards, cabinets, and refrigerator for expired food. The life-force energy of your food directly affects your qi, even when it's stored in the kitchen. Remove stale provisions to make space for food with vital qi.

Nine oranges: Keep a bowl of nine fresh oranges (or similar citrus fruit) in your kitchen. Nine is a lucky feng shui number, while oranges bring bright, cleansing, vibrant energy into the home. And yes, you may eat them!

Above Freshly cut flowers are a delightful feng shui addition to any bathroom, bringing in joyful qi.

Opposite Love and cherish the items in your kitchen, as they serve the purpose of nourishing you. They can be matched sets or more eclectic vintage finds.

bathroom

From a feng shui perspective, the bathroom can be problematic. Thousands of years ago, when feng shui was developed, this area was seen to harbor illness and was reserved for disposal and elimination. However, with modern plumbing in most homes, the bathroom can also offer rest, cleansing, and a spa-like retreat.

In feng shui, the water element represents our wealth and resources, and as a place where water and waste flow in and out regularly. It's helpful to attend to the bathroom to prevent finances flowing down the drains, away from the home.

Toilets: Regulate the flow of water element draining out of the home by closing the seat lid of your toilet bowl when not in use.

Repair leaks: Many home repair issues occur in the bathroom because of the plumbing. Take care of any issues and repair water leaks so that your water qi does not drain away your finances.

Plants: Water feeds and nurtures life. Adding a living, green houseplant to your bathroom can utilize the abundance of water in this area to offer growth and invite the healing energy of nature. If your bathroom has no natural light, add the color green, blue, or teal instead.

bedroom

The most private, healing space in the home is your bedroom. It's where you go to slumber, dream, and restore your body, mind, and heart. We spend a third of our lives in bed, so it's a pretty important place. The bedroom is a symbol of you.

Commanding position: Your bed placement is meaningful and should ideally be placed in the commanding position. This means that when you're lying in bed with your back against the headboard, you can see the bedroom door without being directly in front of it (see page 80). Typically, this locates the bed diagonally from the door. A bed in the commanding position creates safety and protection, and allows you to receive qi. If this is impossible based on the layout of your room, you can place a mirror so that while you're in bed you can see the door in the reflection.

Underneath the bed: It's best to have nothing under the bed to allow the qi to flow with ease. If you must have storage, choose soft and sleep-related items like pillows and linens. What you sleep above will influence you. Take note of the energetic quality of the things under your bed.

Support your bed: A rectangular rug underneath or at the foot of the bed offers the qualities of balance, grounding, and self-care. Choose a color that you love, but yellows or earth tones can be especially supportive.

workspace

Many of us now work part- or full-time from home, or at the very least have a space where we respond to emails and work on a laptop. The desk, or workspace, is connected to your career and work in the world. This is true whether you are an entrepreneur, employee, student, retired, or something in between. Like it or not, technology is part of our lives. We connect to the outside world in our private spaces on a daily basis, so how and where this happens in our homes is important.

Commanding position: As with the bed, when sitting down to work there are two things to check. Set yourself up so you are able to see the door or entrance leading into the space without being directly in line with the door or entrance. Whether you have a formal desk or you're at your dining table, do your best to position yourself in command so that you can see all the opportunities coming your way.

Left A solid, stable headboard is recommended if possible. It is like a mountain behind you, supporting and protecting you while you sleep.

High-back chair: A high-back chair is a simple way to provide support for all the ways you show up in the world. It can offer structure and be the mountain behind you.

Protection from devices: Place an energy-absorbing black crystal such as black tourmaline, shungite, or obsidian in your work area to shield your qi from being overwhelmed by electronic devices. It is also helpful to turn off your devices when you don't need them, to support a healthy work-life balance.

Above Adding plants to your workspace supports growth, creativity, and expansive thinking.

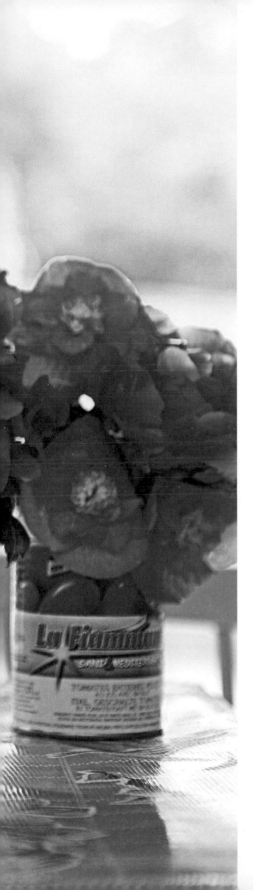

the feng shui of color

- explore color
- color and the five elements
- our favorite colors
- everyday magic ritual: your color circle for healing

explore color

Above In feng shui, color can be used with intention to support, balance, and even create change in your life. Be curious and explore your own color stories.

The everyday magic of color is fundamental to feng shui. Bringing more color into our lives can inspire change and transformation. Color can change your outlook, your qi, and the feel of your home.

Our non-conscious energetic connection to color is deeply rooted in our humanity, and nature is our inspiration. Feng shui is a practice that seeks to harmonize our connection to nature, so it makes sense that we look to the natural world as our teacher when it comes to color. For example, consider the striking impact of a red rose. The bright colors of flowers create a visual reaction that is a beacon to pollinators and humans alike. A fire-engine red outfit can turn many heads in a room.

As you move through this chapter, remember that color can be used for many different applications when it comes to feng shui. Most obviously, you can use color in your home décor; this includes the paint on your walls, the color of furniture, and other accessories and details such as pillows and artwork. We can also use color to shift our personal qi by wearing colors on our body with clothing, jewelry, and cosmetics. Another way to explore color is through play. Maybe throw some paint on a canvas or find new ink colors when you journal or write your grocery list.

three simple ways to explore you own color stories:

· What are you attracted to? What colors do you love? What colors hold memories for you? And what are the stories that arise?

· Take a stroll through nature. How does she express herself with color? What colors are displayed by your most beloved parts of the natural world? What is the color of your favorite flower?

· Examine your home. How does color show up in spaces you spend time in? Look at the built environment around you.

color and the five elements

Feng shui teachings are inspired by the natural world. We live in relationship to nature, and therefore we can learn so much when we look to our environments to inform our lives. Taoist philosophy, one of the roots of feng shui, holds the view that our life force is not static but always shifting from one state to the next. Moving in an unending cycle from growth and vitality to dormant and restful, qi (energetic life force) is exemplified through five basic elements: wood, fire, earth, metal, and water. In feng shui, we understand these elements beyond their physical manifestations like flames, soil, or trees. They are universal energetic essences.

One of the simplest and most effective ways to work with the five elements is through their color associations. Using color in tandem with the meaningful aspects of an element gives us opportunities to move beyond the physical or static. It can connect us with our senses, emotions, and aspirations. We can strategically use color to invite the qualities of the five elements into our homes and lives.

five-element associations

wood

Blue, green, and teal

Growth and healing

fire

Red and fiery oranges

Inspiration and warmth

earth

Yellow and earth tones

Grounding and balance

metal

Gray, white, and metallic

Artistry and precision

water

Black and charcoal

Philosophical and intuitive

Left A floral arrangement is one of our favorite ways to invite in and display the five elements. For instance, wood is found in the green leaves and stems, fiery orange and hot pink bring in fire, the yellow ceramic container is earth, the white blooms are the color of metal, and finally, there is fresh water within the vase.

explore the five element colors in your home

Balance: Bring each of the five elements to harmonize a space. They don't need to be divided up into 20 percent equal parts, as even just an intentional touch of an element can bring things into balance.

Call in an element: If you resonate with or need a bit more of an element, add that color to your home. For instance, if you're focusing on growth in your career, try using wood element colors in your workspace.

Add a new color: Alternatively, notice what colors you shy away from in your home décor. If you almost never have any red or fiery accents, there's an invitation to examine your connection to the fire element. See if there's a way to explore it. Even a small addition of a red flower on your nightstand might begin to shift the qi.

our favorite colors

In this section we have compiled a short list of our favorite colors to help you explore. There are infinite possibilities for each color, so we simply want to give you a place to start.

We also recognize that color is very personal; our fuschia may be your magenta. How we experience color is influenced by so many things—for example, your biology (how your brain and eyes process light and color), the light source (e.g., bright daylight or dim candle light), our cultural background (in traditional Chinese weddings the bride may wear red, where in the West the color is white), our personal experiences, the name of the color, and more.

Our relationship with and understanding of color is nuanced and subjective. Because of this, we have included examples of the colors we had in mind (see pages 34–39).

For our favorite colors, we intentionally chose those that can be linked to nature and objects you can see in the world around you. Please note that in many of the descriptions we refer to "natural pigments" to demonstrate how these colors are connected to the natural world. Traditionally, before chemical processes, colors were created and extracted from the earth. Minerals, rocks, shells, soil, insects, and so on, were ground and cultivated to make natural pigments. We can learn so much when we are curious about where things come from.

On the following pages is a list of colors, their stories, and how they may affect you energetically. We hope these stories help each color to resonate more deeply with you. There is life force or qi in color. Color can offer power and strength, and spark creativity. Color also has the potential to subdue, relax, and inspire reflection—and everything in between. So we encourage you to open up, and use your imagination and intention to create your own magic.

Above Fresh lavender sprigs bring in color energy as well as a soothing aroma that can support sleep and restfulness. This is especially helpful in the bedroom.

reds and pinks

Red is the most powerful and auspicious color in feng shui because it is the color of blood, our life force. Reds and pinks are also associated with love, from passionate to more gentle and caring.

Dragon red is dark and dramatic. The natural pigment of this color is called "dragon's blood," and, like a powerful dragon, it is a strong and vivid force of nature. In feng shui, this tone of red invigorates stagnant or slow qi.

Vermillion is a vibrant red with a touch of orange. The ancient Chinese ground the mineral cinnabar to create this natural pigment. Fiery and energizing, this red is the color of protection in feng shui. The intentional use of even a little vermillion red is said to change your luck.

Fuchsia is a hot pink with a bit of purple mixed in. Fuchsia is vivacious and passionate. Named after the flower, it can be used as an alternative to red to bring more passion and excitement into your life.

Shell pink refers to a pale rosy pink. Sweet and kind, this shade of pink is all about healing the heart. Like the soft and shimmery hue of rose quartz, it symbolizes loving relationships, self-care, and acceptance.

oranges and yellows

In feng shui, tangerines (or other citrus fruits such as oranges, clementines, and satsumas) are symbols of abundance and prosperity because they are gold in color and round like coins. With its similarities to reds and pinks, peach is considered an alluring and seductive color from the feng shui perspective. Yellow tones are grounding, supportive, and offer stability.

Tangerine instantly brings to mind the bright orange fruit. We also use the fragrant peels and essential oils to change the qi of the home. Peel a tangerine and breathe in the uplifting scent!

Peach is a light pink with orange tones. Like shell or soft pink, it is connected to romantic love and relationships, but it can also supercharge your dating life. This color is a combination: passionate, nurturing, and serendipitous. In feng shui, peach blossom luck is the magnetic energy that attracts a partner (or partners!).

Sunflower yellow refers to an expressive and vivid yellow with the yang energy of the sun. This glowing shade of yellow symbolizes strength and power. Also known as "imperial yellow," it was reserved exclusively for the garments of the nobility and ruling classes in ancient China. The sunflower is also a symbol of loyalty because this flower is steadfast in its devotion to the sun.

Yellow ocher is a deep, ferrous yellow. Yellow ocher is also a natural mineral pigment found in artwork as far back as prehistoric times. Iron-rich soil is filtered and dried to produce the color. In feng shui, it represents grounded earth energy. Similarly, you can intentionally use this color in your home to provide support and stability.

greens and blues

The energy of green is creative and expansive, like the height of spring when nature is at its peak. Shades of blue and green embody the wonder of observing birds as they flit from grasses and trees, and soar up toward the bright blue sky.

Deeper blues are connected to spirituality. Medieval and Renaissance painters used lapis lazuli to depict the Virgin Mary's robes, while the Medicine Buddha is always characterized by his blue skin. The natural pigment colors of dark blue are Prussian blue, indigo, and iron blue, which often detail the ocean waves in Japanese woodblock prints.

Grassy green is lush and verdant, capturing the many hues of grasses in a spring meadow. In feng shui, this is the color of innovation and new beginnings, and will move and motivate.

Robin's egg blue, or teal, is a refreshing blue-green that is abundant with vitality, reminding us of springtime and the charming twittering of songbirds. In fact, the color teal is named after a bird. This shade of blue-green is revitalizing and, at the same time, calming and peaceful.

Celestial blue refers to an intense, vivid blue. Historically this color, which is also called lapis lazuli or ultramarine, represented the heavens in religious art. From a feng shui perspective, this healing blue facilitates meditation and your spiritual journey.

Midnight blue is a rich, dark blue with black undertones. The energy of this blue is thoughtful, while cultivating self-awareness and discovery.

purples and browns

Rich purples conjure associations with nobility and splendor. Historically, natural violet pigments were prized for their purity and rarity, making them accessible only to the wealthy. The redder or warmer variations bring to mind the abundance of fertile soil. In Italian, umber is called *terra d'ombra* which translates to "shadowed earth" and was a favorite of many Renaissance and Baroque artists.

Violet refers to bright and velvety purples. In feng shui, violet and royal purple are connected to wealth and abundance.

Lavender is a serene shade of light to mid-value purple with blue undertones. Like the splendid amethyst crystal, lavender inspires tranquillity and ease. It is also associated with abundance, shifting our money mindset to foster contentment and gratitude.

Blackberry is a very dark—almost black-purple. You might also know it as eggplant or by its French name, aubergine. This color is a great alternative to stark black, to bring both wisdom and abundance into your life.

Umber is a dark to warm brown, whose natural pigment is raw umber. Like the rich earth it comes from, the qi of this hue can ground and stabilize.

neutrals

White symbolizes pure yang energy. You can explore warmer tones like beige, tan, latte, and other sandy colors for a more earthy feeling. Black represents pure yin energy, like the cold, watery depths of a deep ocean or an empty, starless midnight sky.

Zinc white is a clean white without any color tint. Zinc oxide, the natural pigment, starts as a solid metal that is ignited at a very high heat until it transforms into a pure white powder. In feng shui, the energy of white is cold, rigid, and contracting, and represents completion and resolution.

Cream includes warm or chalky whites, with some tiny yellow or pink undertones. Minerals such as chalk and limestone are the base of many off-white pigments. These warmer whites have cooling qi with a touch of nurturing earthiness. From a feng shui perspective, creamy neutrals also enable spaciousness, precision, and productivity.

Black onyx is a pure, dense black, like its namesake or volcanic obsidian glass. It is the blackest of blacks. In feng shui, this color is connected to insight, inner wisdom, and the unconscious mind.

Charcoal refers to sooty blacks and very dark gray. Unlike pure black, this color tends to have texture and dimension. The natural pigment for this color is typically made from burned organic material like wood. It has been used by artists for thousands of years. With similar energetic qualities, charcoal is a versatile alternative to black.

metallics

Like the yang energy of the sun, gold is powerful and strong. Like the waxing and waning energy of the yin moon, silver shifts from gray and tarnished to a clear, shimmering white.

Silver is cool and glowing, one of the noble metals. The act of polishing silver is symbolic of clearing away dark clouds to reveal the unseen and hidden brilliance that was always underneath.

Gold is warm and brilliant: *the* symbol of wealth and abundance. It does not tarnish or rust. When gold is burnished to a high sheen, it radiates as if magically lit from within.

your color circle for healing

One of the less obvious ways of working with feng shui is to adorn yourself with color. In Buddhism, there is a tradition of wearing a red string around your wrist to symbolize the receipt of blessings. The circle that is created with a bracelet represents endless continuity and ease (there are no sharp edges), as well as blessings from heaven.

We invite you to create your own color circle for healing. Select a color that embodies the energy you want to create, based on all you have learned about color in this chapter.

1 Find some string, thin ribbon, or cord in your color of choice and cut it to a length of 9in or 27cm. Nine is an auspicious feng shui number because it is the final numeral and represents completion. Expose your string to the light of the sun and the moon—for example, place it on a well-lit windowsill for 24 hours.

2 The next day, tie the bracelet to your wrist with the intention in mind that you've created your magic color circle for healing. You may choose the left wrist if you would like to receive the healing, and the right wrist if you would like to offer healing to others.

3 In time, your color circle for healing will fall apart. If you still have the string, you can burn it in the flame of a candle and offer humble gratitude for its service to you. Disposing of ritual objects with intention and care is preferable as it is a way of acknowledging our ritual as well as closing the circle. It is easy to mindlessly discard what we don't want in the trash, but a careful farewell can be powerful.

4 Whenever it feels appropriate you can create a new circle. Feel free to also explore other colors and materials (like flowers), as well as other intentions.

Opposite Your color circle for healing can be a simple garland of fresh flowers. Natural materials, like flowers, also impart their gifts through fragrance.

the bagua mandala

- the mandala as a divination tool
- the bagua mandala
- the nine areas of the bagua mandala
- everyday magic ritual: your bagua mandala card spread
- your bedroom bagua mandala
- exploring the bagua mandala

the mandala as a divination tool

Above Orange is a color that embodies both earth and fire elements. The brighter orange vase is more firey, while the darker orange bird figurine is earthier.

Feng shui has many instruments of magic that have the power to reveal what your home is telling you. One of these tools is called the bagua, which is the feng shui mandala. The bagua mandala invites you to see your home and environment with more than just your eyes to reveal patterns, obstacles, and even untapped potential. It is an ancient framework that can show you parts of your life that may need more attention. For many of us, it can be difficult to put into words what may be holding us back. It can also be hard to see opportunities that are available and present in our lives. Self-awareness is not always easy, but how great is it that feng shui has tools and techniques that allow you to tap into a deeper realm of wisdom? The magical feng shui mandala is a guide that offers direction on the steps to take toward meaningful transformations, large and small.

The bagua is an Asian divination tool that evolved over thousands of years. Its visual symbolic form, shape, and expression varies. It's typically and most simply depicted as a square grid, but you can also find the feng shui mandala illustrated as a spiral sequence, an octagon, a circle divided into eight pie slices, and so on. Regardless of its diagrammatic appearance, the meaning and application of the bagua is boundless and flexible. The bagua mandala is a metaphysical roadmap with the potential to reveal wisdom and insight for living more mindfully. On the following pages, we'll teach you about this ancient mandala and how to work with it to unveil the magic in your home.

Right Mandalas are found in many cultures. We encourage you to explore the symbols within your own spiritual and cultural lineages with appreciation and respect.

what is a mandala?

A mandala is a visual representation of a journey. You may be familiar with mandalas as an Asian art form and spiritual symbol. In Buddhist art, mandalas have been used for centuries to contemplate unseen celestial realms. Mandalas use form, color, and shape to describe hidden realities. In addition, mandalas are not only two-dimensional. Ancient temples were often constructed as three-dimensional manifestations of a mandala. One simple way to understand a mandala beyond a flat image is to visualize yourself standing in an open space, and noticing all the directions around you. There's your front and back, your left and right, as well as above and below. In feng shui we have our own mandala called the bagua. We also overlay this mandala on a floor plan, which is a two-dimensional representation of your three-dimensional home. The bagua is sometimes also referred to as a map or grid, but in our book we will refer to the bagua as a mandala because we appreciate the multi-dimensional references that the term "mandala" invokes.

seeing beyond with symbols

Our teacher Katherine Metz once told us a story about when Professor Lin Yun, our lineage founder, was asked to define the word "gua." After hesitating for a moment, he said, "No one word can describe a gua, the meanings are infinite. My best choice to help you understand now is 'image.'" You have probably heard the adage: "A picture is worth a thousand words." This idea absolutely applies to the bagua mandala. The bagua and each of its sections tell a story, give insight into a stage of life, and often answer and inspire questions you didn't even know needed asking.

The bagua mandala is rooted in ancient Chinese symbolism. Centuries old, these areas of the bagua mandala began as visual representations to encapsulate their essence. Each of the bagua mandala sections correspond to the symbols found in the *I Ching*, also known as *The Book of Changes*. This book is one of the foundational texts from which feng shui draws its wisdom. The *I Ching* is made of trigrams, which are created from three line combinations of a binary code consisting of a solid yang line and a broken yin line. We have included the image of each trigram on our bagua mandala (see page 49). If this piques your interest, we encourage you to study the *I Ching*. Some of our favorite translations include a deeper exploration of the meaning of each bagua mandala area (see Further Reading, page 142).

From the *I Ching*, fast forward to today where you may be familiar with a simplified one-word name connected to each bagua mandala area. We encourage you to be curious beyond the name. In this book, we were especially careful to select words that would be more comprehensive than what you typically see. For example, "kan" is the Chinese name for the area of the bagua mandala connected to the water element. In our bagua mandala we describe it as "Wisdom." You may also see it referenced elsewhere as "Career." All these words describing this area of the bagua mandala are correct. It goes back to our "yes/and" discussion (see page 16).

Feng shui uses symbolic language through shape, color, and image, and is a profound way to learn about yourself. Similar to words, symbols can communicate ideas, express feelings and emotions, and describe situations. In addition, symbols can offer a visual language when words are challenging, or if they do not seem to be enough. Symbols are also simply another form of sending and sharing information. From a feng shui perspective, you can investigate the floor plan of your home using the symbolic language of the bagua mandala.

When you apply the bagua mandala to your own home you will see how the nine areas align with specific parts of your floor plan. This is something that we will explore in depth in the next chapter. The layout, design details, colors, shape, and other physical aspects of your home have symbolic meaning. Your home is a reflection of you and your life. Once you begin to learn what the symbols mean, it opens you up to understand so much more about yourself.

Below The world offers you infinite possibilities to create spirit and symbolism in your home. One simple way to start is with the meaningful objects you already have.

the bagua mandala

Above The meanings of the areas of the bagua mandala are as vast as the varieties of flora and fauna on the planet.

The bagua mandala is made up of parts that combine to create a whole. The parts are discrete but, at the same time, unified. In Chinese, a part of the bagua mandala is called a "gua". There is a center area with eight guas radiating around it. Together and separately, each of the areas (which includes the eight guas and the center) represents and explores the universal laws that have preoccupied humans for centuries. These different guas begin to categorize and examine the basic building blocks of life. Concepts like mother, father, relationships, career, family harmony, and health are included and explored in the bagua mandala design.

As you can see from our bagua mandala diagram (see opposite page), each of the areas has many layers of meaning, symbolism, and associations. We have included the following: a name to summarize the overall energy, the *I Ching* trigram, associated color(s), the shape(s), the associated element, the seasonal connection, and the Chinese zodiac animal(s). Please note there are countless meanings connected to each gua.

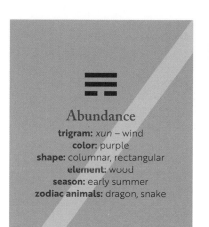

Abundance
trigram: *xun* – wind
color: purple
shape: columnar, rectangular
element: wood
season: early summer
zodiac animals: dragon, snake

Inspiration
trigram: *li* – fire
color: red
shape: triangular
element: fire
season: summer
zodiac animal: horse

Nurture
trigram: *kun* – earth
color: pink
shape: square, flat
element: earth
season: early autumn
zodiac animals: ram, monkey

Growth
trigram: *zhen* – thunder
color: green, teal, blue
shape: columnar, rectangular
element: wood
season: spring
zodiac animal: rabbit

Harmony
symbol: *tai qi* – center
color: yellow
shape: square, flat
element: earth

Reflection
trigram: *dui* – lake
color: white
shape: round
element: metal
season: autumn
zodiac animal: rooster

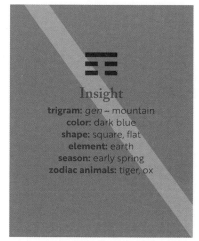

Insight
trigram: *gen* – mountain
color: dark blue
shape: square, flat
element: earth
season: early spring
zodiac animals: tiger, ox

Wisdom
trigram: *kan* – water
color: black
shape: formless, wavy
element: water
season: winter
zodiac animal: rat

Alignment
trigram: *qian* – heaven
color: gray
shape: round
element: metal
season: early winter
zodiac animal: dog, pig

ALIGN WITH THE ENTRANCE WALL OF YOUR SPACE

the nine areas of the bagua mandala

In this section, we'll dive deeply into each of the nine areas so you can understand the language of the bagua mandala.

☵ wisdom *kan*

Tap into your intuition with deep listening: The energy of this area is cool, dark, and thoughtful. It represents boundless possibilities. This gua calls upon the resourceful nature of water and its ability to flow around obstacles, even molding difficult situations into opportunities. While this area is often summed up with the word "career," you may want to think about it on a deeper level. This gua is connected to profound understanding and the wisdom you have to offer the world. Yes, this may be linked to your work, but it can also embody your purpose or calling. These gifts may be intuitive, lying dormant under the surface like a seed in winter.

The essence of the Wisdom gua: I can flow like water and find my own path. I contain all the wisdom I need within me.

Left A feng shui adjustment to increase vitality and boost the qi: place three, five, or nine new, healthy, living plants throughout the home.

☶ insight *gen*

Be still to move forward: The energy of this area is thoughtful, still, and calm. The Insight gua encourages exploration of our inner wells of strength and resolve. When feeling low and unsure, this area reminds us to draw inspiration from the symbol of a mountain. Like a mountain, which is stable and strong, we stand tall with the soles of our feet connected to the earth. Stillness, contemplation, and silence allow space for meaningful insight. Sometimes it's appropriate and helpful to stop, rest, and consider the next steps to take. Perhaps we can ponder what may be holding us back. Is it self-doubt or worry? Or is it time to change course? Meditate from atop your metaphoric mountain to gain perspective and see what skills and knowledge are necessary to move forward.

The essence of the Insight gua: I am a mountain. I can learn about myself through stability and stillness.

☳ growth *zhen*

Activate and kickstart your pioneering spirit: The energy of this area is active, kinetic, and peppy. It represents vitality and innovation, like an intrepid dandelion pushing through a crack in concrete. Growth has many facets, but it is helpful to refer back to its ancient source and symbolism, thunder. A clap of thunder is short, but potent.

The nature of this area is fast and fleeting, a spark that marks the beginning of something amazing. It can help you to create a fresh perspective and gives support when you need to start over and begin again.

The essence of the Growth gua: I can choose when to begin again. I have the potential for growth at any time.

☴ abundance *xun*

Embrace your ability to build true wealth: The energy of this area is gentle, steady, and established. It represents consistent growth, like a mature oak tree with roots that penetrate deeply into the soil. This area encourages you to think of wealth as broader and separate from just money. Abundance and building wealth is the result of gradual and persistent effort. In addition, true wealth includes the generosity that arises when you are overflowing with abundance. The *I Ching* symbol for this gua is called wind. Wind over time can slowly and steadily shape its environment. Like the wind, you also hold the tools to mold your world and accrue wealth with patience, skill, and dedication.

The essence of the Abundance gua: Like the wind, I shape the world I want. Step by step I am creating abundance.

Opposite Pillows and cushions not only provide softness but are also a versatile way to add color and shape to any room in your home.

☲ inspiration *li*

Clarity is your path to success: The energy of this area is bright, revealing, and full of light. It is like opening the shades in a room that has been dark and cold for too long. The sun beams in, revealing what has been hidden or ignored. Are you ready to be seen? What does your heart desire when the spotlight chooses you? Inspiration is the sun shining upon you. The fiery, sometimes unpredictable energy of this area may be overwhelming, but it can also be enlightening. Welcome what you have learned, and mindfully step into success.

The essence of the Inspiration gua: I am ready to be seen. My gifts are recognized and appreciated.

☷ nurture *kun*

Be gentle, open, and vulnerable to receive true love: The energy of this area is soft, receptive, and loving. Allow your heart to open with a vulnerability that can receive a seed that is ready to grow. This area is often connected to romantic partnerships, but it is also about self-acceptance and being available. We are encouraged to contemplate a softer, gentler approach in all of our personal relationships, including the one we have with ourselves. What if we focused on investing our attention and love toward ourselves first? An immersive, feminine, yin energy, Nurture invites us to be kind and loving to ourselves and others.

The essence of the Nurture gua: I belong, I am perfect as I am, and nothing needs fixing. I am supported and loved.

☱ reflection *dui*

Open communication for productive results:
The energy of this area is joyful, rewarding, and content. It is the golden hour, sitting at the edge of a beautifully still lake that mirrors the setting sun, while enjoying deep and meaningful discussions with friends. The Reflection area is also concerned with projects, goals, and creative endeavors coming to fruition. Are you set up for success? Can you complete things in an effective way? Is honest communication needed to find a resolution? Seek support to harvest and celebrate all your hard work.

The essence of the Reflection gua: I am joyful in what I create. I am content and have tremendous gratitude.

 alignment *qian*

Manifest and alchemize your opportunities:
The energy of this area is strong, powerful, and creative. The Alignment gua connects us to the magic and influence of the heavens. Like a bird in the sky, you have a clear view of the way forward. As above, so below, you will envision what is possible and then manifest it. This area is not only about having the support you need to succeed, but also about being in the right place at the right time. Are you seeing the opportunities presented? Pay attention to what the universe offers. For example, a helpful person arrives at a critical time in your life or a small, unassuming event cascades into a big win. The synchronistic, masculine yang energy of Alignment creates opportunities for success and good fortune.

The essence of the Alignment gua: I am powerful. I am supported by benefactors in my life.

harmony *tai qi*

Find your center and welcome peace: The heart of the bagua mandala is the meeting point of the eight guas, representing unity and overall well-being. Like Earth's gravity, Harmony holds, heals, and supports our qi so we don't float away. The physical center of your home is also its energetic center. Like the hub of a wheel, all parts of your life are connected here. The center is a place where you can cultivate stability, peace, and resilience. When you don't know where to turn or what to do next, find your center. It is the container for all the things we cannot put into words and the parts of our life that don't fit into nice little boxes.

The essence of the Harmony gua: I am still and at ease. There is balance and peace within my heart.

Opposite Activate the center of your home for overall health and well-being with the color yellow.

your bagua mandala card spread

Feng shui complements many divination practices, including cartomancy (divination with a deck of cards). If you enjoy working with the Tarot or oracle cards, try this simple nine-card spread based on the bagua mandala. Combine the energetic power and strength of cartomancy with the magic of feng shui to reveal deeper insights into your life.

1 Select your oracle or Tarot deck of choice. It is helpful to be familiar with the symbolism and meaning connected to the deck you are working with, but you can also simply apply your intuition. Regardless, find inspiration in the symbols, images, and colors depicted on the cards.

2 Take nine slow inhales and exhales. Connect with your qi, your inner wisdom, and the energy of your home. Hold this energetic intention as you shuffle the cards.

3 Following the diagram opposite, place each card starting with card 1, Growth. This first card placement represents new beginnings, a perfect starting point for the spread. Continue to lay the cards clockwise as shown, finishing by laying the last card in the center position (card 9, Harmony).

4 When you are ready to read the cards, simply flip them in no particular order. Open your heart to the messages and knowledge you are offered. We suggest you review each card and how it informs the associated meaning. We also encourage you to explore and observe how the card may offer a new perspective on your home's feng shui.

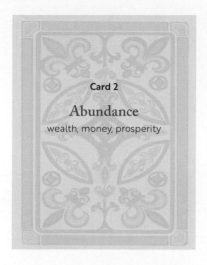

Card 2

Abundance

wealth, money, prosperity

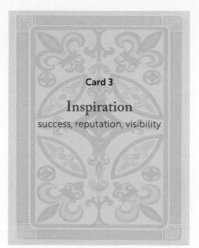

Card 3

Inspiration

success, reputation, visibility

Card 4

Nurture

romantic and intimate
relationships, self-care,
and acceptance

Card 1

Growth

new beginnings, starting
over, family

Card 9

Harmony

overall well-being, balance, health

Card 5

Reflection

communication, productivity,
children (and offspring of
any kind)

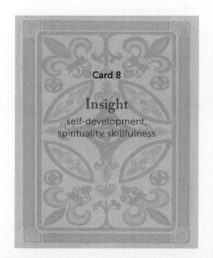

Card 8

Insight

self-development,
spirituality, skillfulness

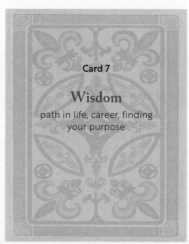

Card 7

Wisdom

path in life, career, finding
your purpose

Card 6

Alignment

helpful people, support
systems, manifestation

your bedroom bagua mandala

Now that you've been introduced to the bagua mandala, we hope you are beginning to feel comfortable exploring it to activate different aspects of your life. The next step is to learn how to work with this magical tool.

starting simple: your bedroom

We'll begin with the bedroom before we move onto whole-home floor plans. As we mentioned in chapter 1, the bedroom is one of the most important rooms in your home, which makes it a great place to start when learning to use the bagua mandala.

1 Begin by identifying the main doorway to your bedroom. You'll find that the door will be located in one or more of these areas: Insight, Wisdom, or Alignment. See the examples opposite. The key to applying the bagua mandala of your bedroom is to remember that the orientation of the bagua mandala is based on the main door to your bedroom. The bottom of the mandala aligns with the entry wall of the room.

2 The next step is to divide the bedroom into a three-by-three grid, corresponding to the nine areas of the bagua mandala. One option is to create a simple drawing of your bedroom like our diagrams. Another option is to stand in the doorway of your bedroom, looking in. The far-right corner will be Nurture, far-left corner Abundance, and so on.

Above Uplift the life-force energy of your bedroom by opening your windows to let in fresh air as often as you can.

Abundance	Inspiration	Nurture
Growth	Harmony	Reflection
Insight	Wisdom	Alignment

ALIGN WITH THE ENTRANCE WALL OF YOUR SPACE

bedroom with door in alignment

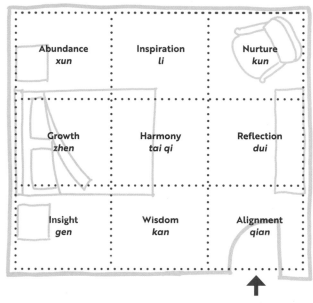

Entrance to room

bedroom with door in insight

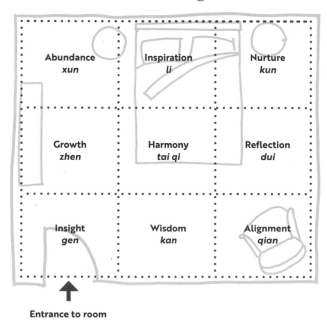

Entrance to room

bedroom with door in wisdom

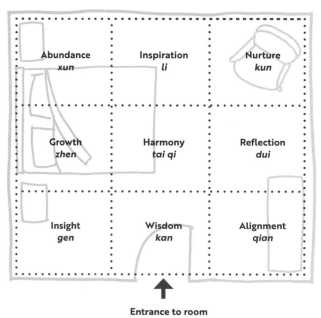

Entrance to room

exploring the bagua mandala

To begin using the bagua mandala, please note an important guideline: Select only one, two, or three areas to adjust. Then apply just one or two suggestions that resonate with you. Explore the most pertinent and relevant areas and move forward with thoughtful intention.

We offer a variety of feng shui adjustments and include many that do not require you to have a floor plan. If you do want to work with your floor plan, you can refer to chapter 4. As a reminder, it's also equally as effective to explore the bagua mandala of your bedroom. Below are three general ways to explore any bagua mandala area in your home's feng shui.

three ways

Color: Bring the color connected to the gua into any area of your home. You can also find the corresponding area of your bedroom or entire home and apply the color there.

Shape: Check out the shape associated with the gua you want to enhance and include it in the décor of any area of your home. You can also find the corresponding area of your bedroom or entire home and apply the shape there. Some examples include a vase that is columnar, a pattern with triangles, or a flat rug.

Stir up the qi: Bring some fresh qi into the corresponding area of your bedroom or entire home by giving it some attention. For instance, decluttering, dusting, or even just spending more time in that area can move the energy.

The following pages offer additional specific ways to connect and embody each area of the bagua mandala. Some are best applied to the specific area in your bedroom (page 58), or using your home's floor plan (Chapter 4). We have also provided you with simple ways to bring the intention and qi of each area into your overall environment, with no floor plan required. Remember, take it step by step and work with up to three areas and only a couple of suggestions.

wisdom *kan*

Career, path in life, ancestors

Flow: Add imagery of water or water elements—perhaps a fountain—to the Wisdom area of your home. If the object has water, like a fountain, be mindful to maintain it and keep it clean and in good working condition.

Expand: Hang a mirror in the Wisdom area in your home or bedroom.

Observe: Fill a shallow bowl with clean drinking water. Slowly meander around your home with the bowl of water, taking care not to spill any. As you move about your home, observe the waves, ripples, and subtle movements in the water. Notice how the water shifts, rises, and falls. When you feel the exercise is complete, find a quiet place to stop. Sit and watch the water as it stills. When done, mindfully drink the water.

insight *gen*

Self-cultivation, knowledge, spirituality

Gather: Books are symbols of knowledge. Place favorite books that represent the skills and aspirations for insight that you wish to cultivate in the Insight area in your home or bedroom.

Write: Start a journal dedicated to your self-cultivation, using the color dark blue. The journal itself can be dark blue, or you can use a pen with dark blue ink.

Visualize: Meditation on the mountaintop: Find a comfortable meditation spot. It can be any space you can carve out like on a chair, a meditation cushion, or even perched on the edge of your bed. Visualize sitting on top of a mountain. You

Above Find feng shui inspiration in the everyday items around your home. Books represent knowledge, salt is purifying, and pomegranates invite abundance.

see the landscape rolling out in front of you with a clear, bird's-eye view of everything all around. As you appreciate the vista, take a deep breath in, then slowly exhale. Repeat this breathing nine times. As you complete your ninth resuscitation, visualize a clear pathway down the mountain guiding your way. Finish by gently opening your eyes and returning to your normal breathing.

䷲ growth *zhen*

New beginnings, family, action

Cultivate: Place a new, living, green plant in a black pot. Place this pot in the Growth area in your home for vitality. If you have a green thumb, you can plant a cutting or even try growing something from seed. (Refer to chapter 5 for some plant suggestions!)

Vitality: If you have the space, place nine new, living, green plants throughout your home. They need not be the same type of plant. However, you should thread them together energetically and visually. You can do this by using the same type of planter, the same color pot, or simply by tying a red ribbon around each plant (either around the pot or loosely around a stem).

Explore: Take inspiration from the natural world around you. Go for a walk and find an example of a resilient plant that is growing in spite of its surroundings: vines that wind through a fence, grass that pushes up through cracks in the asphalt, or shoots of new growth on a weathered, aged tree stump.

䷸ abundance *xun*

Wealth, prosperity, self-worth

Invite: Fruit symbolizes wealth and abundance. Place a bowl with nine pieces of your favorite fresh fruit in any area of your home. Yes, you can eat the fruit! The number nine symbolizes the auspicious feng shui number of completion.

Cultivate: This area is connected to the imagery of the tree. Add a photo or representation of a tree in the Abundance area in your home or bedroom with the intention to build wealth like the deep roots of a tree.

Intention: Coins also symbolize abundance. Every day for 27 days, place a coin in a red box. Each time you add another coin, set an intention to be patient and kind to yourself with regards to saving and building wealth in your life. At the end of the 27 days, practice generosity by offering a financial donation to a good cause or surprise a friend by treating them to coffee.

Above Abundance can be defined as having a generous bowl of fruit to share with your neighbors.

Left Many fresh green cuttings can thrive and even start to root when placed in a container of clean water. These plant babies can also offer the qi of growth and new beginnings.

☲ inspiration *li*

Fame, reputation, visibility

Brighten: Check all the light fixtures in your home. Lighting is connected to this gua. Take care that all the lights are functional and working properly.

Glow: Candles are also connected to the fiery nature of the Inspiration area. Place candles in the areas of your home that could use more warmth and light.

Shine: Add an additional light fixture or candle to your desk or workspace, with the intention to bring more visibility to your career and work life.

☷ nurture *kun*

Partnership, romance, the mother

Pair up: Find a pair of new, living, green plants and pot them up in one planter. Place this in the Nurture area in your home or bedroom. Choose a plant that is easy to care for, with heart-shaped leaves. A great choice is two orchid plants in one pot. (Refer to chapter 5 for some plant suggestions!)

Envision: Add imagery that represents the love that you are open to receiving. One example is whimsical artwork of a loving couple. You could also have a pair of matching pieces of art. Place the imagery in the Nurture area in your home or bedroom.

Intention: Find one or two pink crystals or stones to place on your nightstand. One piece for self-love, two for romantic partnership. We love rhodonite to promote self-love, kindness, and self-care, especially after a tough breakup. Rose quartz is also a favorite to invite new love, support existing love, or help to heal a broken heart.

Above Candles bring in fire element. They can be any size and color. Alternatively, twinkle lights and flameless battery-operated candles work as well.

exploring the bagua mandala **63**

Above Whether you are using a new or pre-existing mirror to enhance your feng shui, be sure to set a clear intention.

☱ reflection *dui*

Completion, children, joy

Enhance: Hang a round mirror in the Reflection area in your home or bedroom, with the intention to bring more joy and contemplation into your life.

Gather: Add a white bowl or box to any room in your home. Feel free to place photographs inside, or other symbolic objects that bring you joy, or for which you have gratitude.

Visualize: Choose something in your life that you would like to see resolved, like a project that needs a little push to reach completion. Ring a metal bell nine times while setting an intention and visualizing the outcome of this wish. Take your time while ringing the bell. Listen and feel the reverberations of each sound. Wait until each ring's vibrations are complete before moving on to the next.

☰ alignment *qian*

Benefactors, travel, the father

Invite: Ring a metal bell, wind chime, or singing bowl as you walk around your home. Start at the front door, hugging the wall on your left, with the intention that you are calling in and inviting supportive qi into your life.

Activate: Add a wind chime to the Alignment area of your home or bedroom to activate and enhance movement so you can receive from benefactors.

Intention: Write a list of nine ways you will become a more helpful person to your family, friends, and colleagues. Keep it simple. Place this list in a small metal box or silver-colored envelope located in the Alignment area of your home or bedroom.

 ## harmony *tai qi*

Overall health and well-being, balance

Nature: Place a bouquet of yellow flowers, a bowl of lemons, or any other yellow item from nature in the center of your living room.

Sparkle: Hang a feng shui crystal ball from the ceiling, centered above your bed. Visualize that it is the sun shining upon you, calling in joy and harmony. A feng shui crystal ball is a human-made, faceted, spherical prism made of crystal glass. We recommend using one that is 1½in (40mm) or larger in diameter (see Resources, page 140).

Breathe: Sit in the center of your favorite room in your home. With mindful intention, place your hands on your heart while slowly breathing in and out nine times. Take a long inhale and receive the air from the space around you. Pause, then allow yourself a full exhale while noticing your breath and how it intermingles with your environment.

Above Vibrant like the sun, fresh lemons cleanse, revitalize, and stimulate your qi.

reading your floor plan

- reveal the mandala of your home
- floor plan 1: missing areas
- floor plan 2: extensions
- floor plan 3: garages and secondary doors
- floor plan 4: commanding position
- floor plan 5: small homes

reveal the mandala of your home

Now that you've been introduced to the bagua mandala in chapter 3, we hope you are beginning to feel comfortable exploring it to activate different aspects of your life. The next step is to learn how to apply this magical tool to your own home's floor plan.

The bagua mandala can be overlaid on the bedroom (see page 58), as well as the entire home. In the following pages, we will teach you how to apply the bagua mandala to your primary floor plan. In addition we'll dive in deeper and teach some ways to read the qi of your home in five real-life feng shui floor plan examples.

To begin, you will learn how to overlay the mandala on your primary floor plan. You will need to create a drawing or sketch, or use an existing builder's plan if you have access to one.

1 Locate the formal front door of the home.

2 Rotate the floor plan so the front-door wall aligns with the bottom of the bagua mandala (Insight, Wisdom, and Alignment areas).

3 Overlay a three-by-three grid that is proportional to the floor plan. Imagine the mandala is a transparent piece of plastic wrap that stretches from the front-door wall, out toward the back wall and then out to both sides of the home. Congratulations, you have revealed your home's bagua mandala!

the spaces you live in

In this book, we focus on the primary floor plan: where most of the living spaces are on the same level as the front door. The main living spaces, such as the kitchen, living room, and bedrooms, are the most important when reviewing the feng shui of a home. Why? Because you spend the most time in these areas of the home.

If your home's floor plan is different or unique, this is considered a complicated layout. What about upper floors, attics, and basements? We recommend you apply the bagua mandala on the occupied bedrooms, room-by-room.

It's helpful to work with a correctly measured floor plan and there are numerous resources, how-to guides, and apps available on the internet to assist in creating your floor plan drawing. In feng shui your intention and effort is powerful, so do your best when creating a drawing or floor plan sketch. Remember, you can keep it simple and work with the most influential bagua mandala—your bedroom's (see page 58).

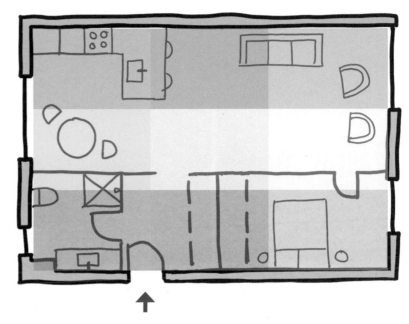

Abundance	Inspiration	Nurture
Growth	Harmony	Reflection
Insight	Wisdom	Alignment

**ALIGN WITH THE
ENTRANCE WALL OF YOUR SPACE**

reading the qi of your home

Many of us learn best by example. This is why we've offered five floor plans to teach you how to read your home's mandala layout. These floor plans introduce important feng shui concepts and design details, as well as simple feng shui adjustments. Our five selected floor plans are gestural and are not intended to be a perfect fit. Our readings are not exhaustive, but instead highlight what is most helpful. However, we are confident each reader will walk away with practical feng shui teachings that apply to their own home.

Right Notice the colors within your home and even your wardrobe. They are energetically connected to you and can teach you about your own personal qi.

floor plan 1: missing areas

Above Flat, rectangular-shaped rugs are earth element, while striped patterns beckon wood element. Dark blue and black accents are water, red flowers are fire, and finally white walls and furniture brings in metal element.

For our first floor plan, we will review "missing areas." This can occur when a home or room's layout creates a void or missing part of the bagua mandala.

The position of the front door and the home's shape may create voids or missing areas as seen in the example opposite. As we can see in this plan, the position of the front entrance creates missing areas in Insight and Alignment. Complex shapes beyond a simple square or rectangle will generate missing areas and/or extensions in the bagua mandala. In this plan, part of Nurture is missing due to the irregular shape of the house. It's a "missing area" if it is less than half of the overall depth and/or width of the home.

A missing bagua mandala area may sound troubling. However, while missing areas may indicate areas in your life where you need more qi, this awareness and insight is also a gift. You now know which parts of your life may require attention. It does *not* mean that you must move, or that your house has "bad feng shui." Instead, a missing area is a golden opportunity to see where you could benefit from an energy boost. Feng shui adjustments can offer support to enhance missing bagua mandala areas, which highlight the undernourished aspects of our energetic life. On page 72 we offer three basic ways to correct a missing area.

Ready, set, and here we go for our first floor plan reading! Let's review missing areas.

1A: Missing area in Insight:

The Insight area is partially missing, which may indicate the need to focus on self-cultivation and personal growth work. A large, square mirror on the wall (indicated by the red line on the plan, opposite) will expand the view and qi for the missing area, while the square shape supports the earth element connected to Insight.

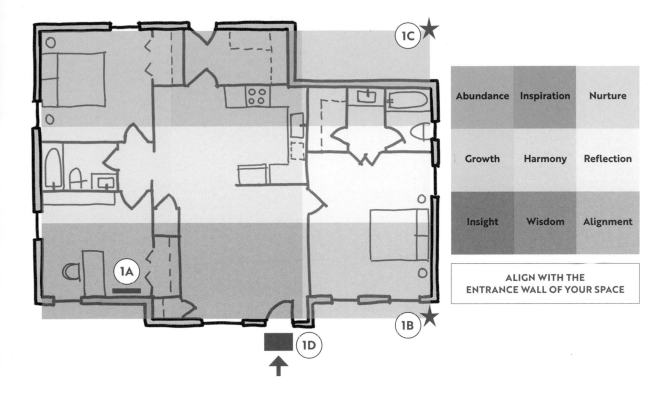

Abundance	Inspiration	Nurture
Growth	Harmony	Reflection
Insight	Wisdom	Alignment

ALIGN WITH THE ENTRANCE WALL OF YOUR SPACE

1B: Missing area in Alignment:

The Alignment area also has a portion missing. This may point to challenges with finding supportive, helpful people. The inhabitants can bring in fresh qi and benefactors to their life by hanging a metal wind chime right outside the house in the corner indicated by the red star (see above). Alternatively, if there is no access to the outdoor space, ring a bell in this corner of the home nine times to call in supportive people and good fortune, as often as needed.

1C: Missing area in Nurture:

Almost half of the Nurture area is missing on this bagua mandala, indicating challenges in partnerships of all kinds. As this is a house, the inhabitant might plant a tree in the corner indicated by the red star (see above), or plant flowers and/or shrubs in the missing area.

Plants offer life qi to the weakened bagua mandala area. They can also set an intention for romantic relationships to thrive and grow.

1D: Activate Wisdom:

The front door is *always* where we lay the bottom of the bagua mandala. In this particular floor plan, the entry is in Wisdom. The door in Wisdom may indicate that the inhabitants have a straightforward way to welcome work and friendships. And if they need a bit more support in their careers, a black welcome mat indicated by the red rectangle (see above) will enhance and draw in wisdom and opportunities in all areas of their life.

three simple ways to adjust a missing area

Select *only one* of the suggestions below. Let the universe know that you are focused and trust the chosen feng shui adjustment. We've offered three of the most helpful and easy-to-implement options, but there are always more ways. One is not better than another.

Add color connected to the area: This can be achieved by painting the wall along the missing area. You can also bring in color with substantial and strong home décor additions, like large artwork or window treatments.

Add plants for more life qi: Place the plants along the interior of the wall in the missing area. If you have access to the exterior, shrubbery or ideally a tree may be planted to invite the energy into the missing area.

Add a mirror. Mirrors are powerful feng shui objects. In the case of missing areas, hang a flat, unobscured mirror on the wall along the missing area to strategically invite qi as well as expand the space to reclaim the missing area. Ideally, the mirror should be as large as possible, but even a small, 3in (7.5cm) round mirror with a clear intention can be effective.

floor plan 2: extensions

In feng shui we have what are called "extensions" or "projections," when the shape of the home creates "more" of a particular bagua mandala area. Generally, an extension is a part of the home that extends out and is less than half the overall width of the entire home. These feng shui concepts of missing areas and extensions can be challenging to understand, which is why we use visual examples like floor plan 2 (see page 75), which has an extension in Inspiration.

Most people think that more is more. In general, an extension may indicate an enhancement, or more qi to attribute to that area of the bagua mandala. And indeed, unlike missing areas, typically there is no need to adjust a small extension. It's an energetic bonus and enhancement in that part of your life. However, when there is a large extension that is out of proportion with the rest of the bagua mandala, it is often helpful to see if there is also a similar imbalance playing out in that area of your life. The good news is that large extensions can be balanced and supported with feng shui adjustments.

Above The metal element is strong when there is an abundance of white and light gray. The water element is seen in the black accents, wood is in the fresh green botanicals, candles bring in fire, and finally the earth element is found in the brown wood table and stools.

Left A mirror placed over a fireplace in the Abundance area can balance any excess fire element. In addition, the square black frame brings in a touch of water to support further.

adjusting an out-of-balance extension

1 First examine, unpack, and ask how this imbalance shows up in your life. Sometimes, the large extension is not a problem but may, in fact, be supportive. In this case, no feng shui adjustment is required.

2 If there is an adjustment required, set an intention to adjust the imbalance uncovered in step 1.

3 One of the simplest ways to harmonize a very large and unbalanced extension is five element color theory. Below is a chart with corresponding elemental color adjustments for the out-of-balance extension. Simply add one (or more) of these elemental colors to the room with intention. You're also invited to wear the color and see how the color shows up in other areas of your life.

	a softer, more gentle approach makes the imbalance more useful	create a dramatic and drastic shift, cutting through the issue
wisdom	**wood** (blue, green, and teal)	**earth** (yellow and earth tones)
nurture	**metal** (gray, white, and metallics)	**wood** (blue, green, and teal)
growth	**fire** (red and fiery oranges)	**metal** (gray, white, and metallics)
abundance	**fire** (red and fiery oranges)	**metal** (gray, white, and metallics)
alignment	**water** (black and charcoal)	**fire** (red and fiery oranges)
reflection	**water** (black and charcoal)	**fire** (red and fiery oranges)
insight	**metal** (gray, white, and metallics)	**wood** (blue, green, and teal)
inspiration	**earth** (yellow and earth tones)	**water** (black and charcoal)
harmony	**metal** (gray, white, and metallics)	**wood** (blue, green, and teal)

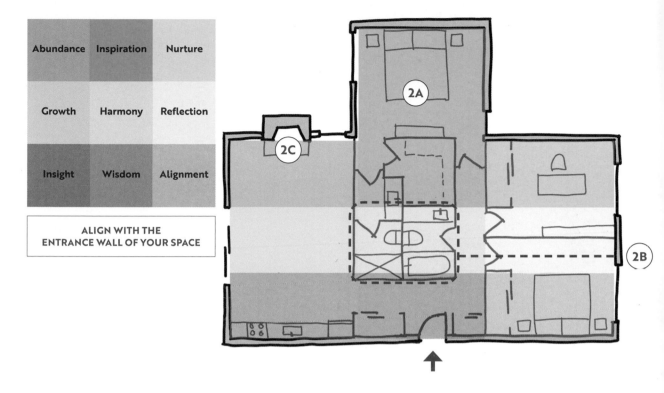

Abundance	Inspiration	Nurture
Growth	Harmony	Reflection
Insight	Wisdom	Alignment

ALIGN WITH THE ENTRANCE WALL OF YOUR SPACE

2A: Large extension in Inspiration:

This is an example of an out-of-balance extension because it almost triples the footprint of the Inspiration area. When you see a large imbalance, look at the qualities of the bagua mandala area. Are the people living here ultra visible, experiencing too much notoriety and publicity? Or do they feel burned out, uninspired, and exhausted? In this situation we would advise water or earth element colors to remedy the bedroom.

2B: Two bathrooms in the center, Harmony:

Aside from extensions, this plan depicts a design detail to look out for: a bathroom in the center of the bagua mandala. Actually, there are two bathrooms! A bathroom in the center of the home's bagua mandala indicates depletion in all areas of the bagua. When you have two bathrooms, the effect multiplies. We recommend the installation of full-length mirrors on the outside (facing the hallway) of both toilet room doors. The mirrors will energetically erase the qi of the bathroom. The larger the mirror, the better.

2C: Fireplace in Abundance:

The last suggestion addresses the fireplace in the Abundance area. Fireplaces produce fire, and the bagua mandala area here is connected to the wood element. A simple addition of some water element adjacent to (or above) the fireplace will energetically cool down the flames that may burn up your finances. This can be achieved with the addition of water element colors, imagery of water, or a large mirror. This adjustment also applies to stoves (or your primary cooking appliance) in the Abundance area.

floor plan 3:
garages and secondary doors

Above A lively, well-kept space adjacent to a secondary exterior door is beneficial because it improves the quality of the qi flowing in and out.

garages

From a feng shui perspective, a garage is like a shipping port for opportunities and resources. A garage door is a large and generous portal for qi, accommodating cars but also delivering abundant resources into the home. Automobiles offer movement, mobility, and a connection to the outside world. For many of us, access to a car is essential for employment, productivity, and a social life.

Since garages are often used as a storage area for things (as well as cars), they can sometimes get cluttered. That is okay. Just be sure to review your storage on a regular basis. If you need assistance from friends, family, or a professional organizer, ask for it! For a feng shui boost, ring a bell in the Alignment area to call in helpful people. Or for a kickstart, set a timer and dedicate nine minutes to organizing the garage.

Garages are included in the overall bagua mandala layout when the walls and roof of the garage are attached to the house or to part of the house.

secondary exterior doors

Besides the "formal" front door, you may have a side or back door. A garage door also qualifies as a secondary door. Secondary exterior doors are not necessarily positive or negative, but rather they are messages from your home to pay attention. All doors, especially exterior doors connecting to the outside world, are portals for qi to enter our spaces. Therefore, we recommend you notice and ask questions about the mandala areas where the secondary exterior doors are located. Is the qi of that area leaking or weakened, or are

there possibilities for more resources to come in? Are you aware of what is coming in and out of that area of your life? The most important areas to pay attention to are to the rear of the mandala: Abundance, Inspiration, and Nurture. These areas are more vulnerable because they are in the back—the hidden, yin side of the home.

The simplest way to strengthen and protect a back door is to attach a bell, so that when it opens, you can hear a clear, distinct sound. We recommend a shopkeeper's bell, but any bell will work. Think of it as a feng shui alarm system, so that you know when qi is coming in or out.

Another note about front doors. We are often asked: "What if I use the side door to enter my house?" In feng shui, when overlaying the bagua mandala, the formal front door is always the front door and always considered the mouth of qi. Even if you usually use a side or garage door when coming and going, we recommend that you make an effort to use your front door on a daily basis to pick up mail, walk the dog, or greet visitors. Open it with intention to receive new opportunities and qi.

Above The formal front door is essential to your home's feng shui. Aim to open it daily, to invite fresh qi into your home and life.

3A: Secondary door in Nurture:

The back door of the garage (and side door into the home from the garage) may encourage unsolicited feedback from others, regarding relationships within the home. Placing a bell on each door will help to keep nosy people at a distance.

3B: Secondary door in Inspiration:

This floor plan has a back door in the bagua mandala area related to one's reputation. Is someone talking behind the inhabitant's back and gossiping about them? Again, attaching a bell to the secondary door will protect and adjust the qi in this part of their life.

3C: Stove in Abundance:

Depending on where they are located, stoves, primary cooking appliances, and fireplaces can "burn up" the qi. The bagua mandala areas where you want to correct these fiery spots are Growth, Abundance, Harmony, Alignment, and Reflection. Balance the fire by adding water element colors or a mirror to cool down the flames.

3D: Missing area in Alignment:

A portion of Alignment is missing. Paint the garage door gray, the color of Alignment (or see page 30–39 for more ideas). As a plus, a garage door in this area can mean that this family connects with helpful and supportive people more easily.

Left From a feng shui perspective, fireplaces and stoves are cozy spots to gather the qi of warmth and generosity.

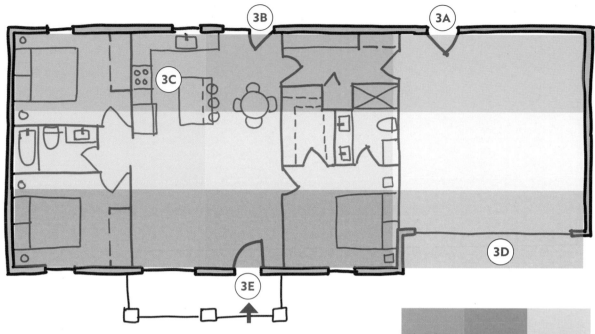

3E: Front and back door alignment:

Take care to avoid a clear and unobstructed view of the back door when standing at the front door looking in. Imagine qi entering the front door and then being drawn straight out the back, rather than graciously circulating and flowing within the home. This design may affect the occupants' ability to maintain resources, leaving them feeling energetically depleted.

One way to adjust this front and back door alignment is skillfully illustrated in this floor plan with the placement of the dining table in the line of qi. Well-placed furniture adjusts the movement of qi around the space. Another way to redirect the energy is with a faceted, feng shui crystal ball (see page 65) hung from the ceiling somewhere in that line between the two doors.

Abundance	Inspiration	Nurture
Growth	Harmony	Reflection
Insight	Wisdom	Alignment

**ALIGN WITH THE
ENTRANCE WALL OF YOUR SPACE**

floor plan 4: commanding position

Above Use your stove daily, even just to boil water for tea. Set the intention to ignite the positive qualities of the fire element each day.

The commanding position is a feng shui principle that everyone can benefit from. It offers guidance on creating the most advantageous position in three key aspects of life: your personal well-being, work life, and resources. These correspond energetically to three areas of your home respectively: your bed, desk, and stove (or primary cooking appliance). The commanding position may seem like simple common sense, but it still greatly impacts your life and qi. When you're out of command, you may experience missed opportunities, increased anxiety, and restless sleep. Not being in the commanding position may cause mishaps, a lack of control and protection, and can ultimately drain your energy.

In this floor plan (see page 83) we will review how to locate your bed, desk, and stove in the commanding position to benefit from the best flow of qi. Ideally, your bed, desk, and stove should be positioned so when you are laying in bed, sitting at your computer, or standing cooking, you can see the door or entry into the room. This floor plan illustrates all three "in command" of the room or space. In addition, you don't want to be located so that you are directly in the line of qi and aligned with the door.

Right Wall coverings are one way to adjust your feng shui. Select the color, design, and imagery with intention. There's also an opportunity to go big and dramatic, if that's the kind of qi you are looking for.

Whenever possible, it is ideal to move furniture into the commanding position. But what if you can't reposition the bed, desk, or stove? Then honestly ask yourself: Is it that you can't move it or that you don't want to move it? Physically moving your bed or desk into the commanding position offers a perfect opportunity to get out of your comfort zone and gain a new perspective. However, if you truly cannot place your bed, desk, or stove in the commanding position, here are two ways to adjust it:

• If you cannot see the door, set up a mirror so that when you're laying in bed, sitting at your desk, or cooking you can see the reflection of the door in the mirror. This is the best adjustment if your stove, or any other installed cooking appliance, cannot be repositioned.

• If you're in the line of qi when laying in bed, sitting at your desk, or cooking, hang a faceted feng shui crystal ball from the ceiling somewhere between your position and the door.

4A Bed in commanding position:

The bed is where you recharge, sleep, and heal yourself, and therefore represents the most intimate parts of you. Placing your bed in the commanding position creates opportunities for rest and rejuvenation.

4B Desk in commanding position:

Wherever you work, whether from home or in the outside world, try to place your desk in the commanding position which represents your career and path in life. When you are in command of your desk, you have a wide view of all the qi that comes your way, reducing unexpected surprises and challenges.

4C Stove (or primary cooking appliance) in commanding position:

Where you cook your food affects your health and overall well-being. The stove location is the primary area where you cook for yourself and includes gas and electric cooktops. If you don't have a cooktop, but use a small microwave oven or hotplate, this would be your "stove" for this purpose. Where you cook represents your wealth and resources. How well you nourish yourself connects to your success and prosperity. It is common in many homes to see the stove against a wall, placing it out of command, and some kitchens also have a secondary door (see page 76).

Left A brown, solid, wood desk is considered primarily the earth element because of its earthy color and flat, stable shape. It's a recommended desk type for security, balance, and support in your work life.

Abundance	Inspiration	Nurture
Growth	Harmony	Reflection
Insight	Wisdom	Alignment

ALIGN WITH THE ENTRANCE WALL OF YOUR SPACE

4D Balcony in Nurture:

The outdoor balcony shown in this floor plan is a nuance on a missing area (see page 71). As it is still a functional and private space connected to the home, we would say it weakens the bagua mandala area, but it's not missing. However, the inhabitants are advised to strengthen the qi in the area to enhance their partnership and self-care. They can show the terrace some love by creating a vibrant and well-tended space with flowering plants, a colorful outdoor rug, and a pair of chairs to represent each partner.

4E Bathroom in Alignment:

Inhabitants with a bathroom in this area of the bagua mandala may wish to strengthen their support system. To enhance the qi, add color connected to this bagua mandala area with paint, artwork, or other decorative accents like linens or a shower curtain. For example, upgrade to gray-colored bath linens, the color related to Alignment.

floor plan 5: small homes

Above There's room in the practice of feng shui for creative messiness and expression, with no requirement to be minimal, organized, or perfect.

To close this chapter, we want to make sure that we review a small home, like a one-room house or apartment, where everything is—more or less—in one open space. To begin with, yes, you can still apply feng shui principles to a small space. The beauty of feng shui is that you don't need to buy anything, spend a great deal of money, or have a large home.

Even in the smallest of spaces, we recommend creating opportunities for rituals around your sleep, work, and dining times. For instance, if the only place to eat your meals and work from home is while sitting in bed, then take a few moments to make up the bed when you start each day. Set yourself a little placemat at each meal, power down and tuck away your laptop when you're done with work, and arrange your bed to prepare for sleep every night.

5A Missing area in Abundance:
This is a helpful example of a floor plan where it is difficult to tell if there is a missing area in Abundance or an extension in Insight. Which is it? In cases like this, when the difference in dimensions is equal, simply treat it as a missing area (see page 70–72).

5B Desk placement facing a wall:
While this workspace is in the commanding position, the person sitting here faces a wall, which isn't ideal. The person working here may feel like they are hitting a wall at work or may not be able see and execute a long-term vision for their career. One of the best ways to adjust this is to place a mirror on the wall over the desk; this will allow them to expand the possibilities in their work life.

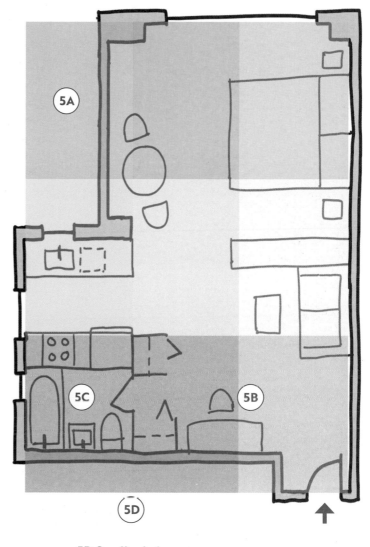

Abundance	Inspiration	Nurture
Growth	Harmony	Reflection
Insight	Wisdom	Alignment

ALIGN WITH THE
ENTRANCE WALL OF YOUR SPACE

5C Bathroom in Insight:

A bathroom in this bagua mandala area may mean that the occupants experience doubt or lack self-confidence. Add living, green plants. The excess water element feeds the wood element, resulting in an increase in upward growth and more life-affirming qi. It is helpful to adjust a bathroom in any of the bagua mandala areas with the suggestions from chapter 1 (see page 25), floor plan 2 (see page 75), and floor plan 4 (see page 83).

5D Small missing areas:

Finally, this plan does have some missing qi in the Insight areas of the bagua mandala. Accordingly, these areas can be adjusted with a houseplant, adding the color of the bagua mandala area, or with a mirror on the wall (see page 72).

the everyday magic of plants

- plant magic
- the houseplant bagua mandala
- everyday magic ritual: a wild garden offering

plant magic

Whether you live in a large house in the country or in a small city apartment, plants are a delightful way to bring magic into your home's feng shui. While houseplants are not required for "good" feng shui, they have the advantage of being relatively accessible. In this chapter, we will review the feng shui magic of plants and how you can use them to enhance and activate the qi in your home.

Plants have always been a way to create harmony between home and nature. The plant world is especially healing for humans. In our modern world, many of us no longer know what it feels like to run our hands through soil and touch the earth. There is magic in connecting with the earth. When you tend to houseplants, there's an unspoken agreement that you are caring for another living being. Plants live and breathe. They require air, sunlight, water, love, and care, just like you. If neglected and ignored, living things will wither away and die. If cared for, they will flourish and grow. So, the plant world offers us gifts and teachings. Houseplants offer a way for us to integrate nature into our everyday home life.

Left When you are sitting at your desk, place a plant in the top-left corner to boost wealth and abundance in your work life.

the houseplant bagua mandala

In earlier chapters we have explored the bagua mandala and how to work with it in your home (see pages 58–65). In this chapter, we offer you a simple way to work with the magic of houseplants. We have assembled our favorite houseplants and organized them to correspond with the bagua mandala.

These plants were selected based on our personal experience, as we care for these plants in our own homes.

three houseplant pro-tips

· Research the requirements of your plant such as the temperature and amount of light it needs, as well as how pet-friendly and easy to care for it is, then find the one that best suits you and your home.

· Connect with your plant friend with sight and touch. Look at the plant to see how it's faring. Check in regularly to see when it needs water. Just stick your finger a few inches into the soil to see if it is dry.

· Start with a forgiving and easy-to-care-for plant, such as pothos (see page 91), or use what is available to you. Always do the best you can within your means.

Below Cultivating plants from seeds or bulbs allows opportunities for deeper connections with the cycles of nature.

shift the qi with houseplants

Activate the area of your home that connects with the bagua mandala by placing the specified houseplant in that area. For example, if you would like to attract more abundance, place the African violet in the Abundance area of your home or bedroom.

If the corresponding bagua mandala area doesn't work because of lighting or other practical reasons, you can place the plant anywhere in the home where it can thrive.

Work with one new plant at a time. Notice and pay attention to the messages you receive after bringing this new friend into your home.

In most cases, it is best to bring in a new houseplant. As with all feng shui adjustments, you want to bring in new qi! Ideally, procure your new plant from a reputable source. You could even ask a friend for a cutting.

Wisdom: Jade succulents resemble wise, old trees in miniature form. Often connected to wealth due to their coin-shaped leaves, we suggest using jade plants to cultivate wisdom because of their ability to store water and energy. Water is connected to wisdom and depth of knowledge.

Insight: Prayer plants are slow-growing and deliberate. They quietly fold their leaves up at night as if in prayer, bringing to mind our own journey of self-discovery. We meditate, pray, and chant to gain insight and a deeper connection with ourselves.

Growth: Pothos are perfect for plant newbies as they're one of the easiest houseplants to care for. Their fast-growing, heart-shaped leaves invite growth and action. Even when neglected, the forgiving pothos will remind you that you always have an opportunity to begin again.

Abundance: The flowers of the African violet are delicate, purple (the color of this bagua mandala area), and bloom in abundance. They are also almost effortless to propagate, and so teach us that we can generously and graciously share our wealth and beauty with the world.

Inspiration: *Oxalis triangularis* is a purple-red plant with triangular leaves (the color and shape of this bagua mandala area). Caring for this plant is relatively easy and it will bring an inspiring, warm energy to any room.

Nurture: We often speak about the orchid's connection to love and partnership. On a deeper level, the orchid also requires love and care in order to flower. We must continue to care for and nurture ourselves and others, even in tough times.

Reflection: With its large, shiny leaves, the fiddle leaf fig is a beautiful statement plant for any room and a joy to watch grow. When given the right conditions fiddle leaf figs can grow quickly. The pear-shaped leaves remind us of the sweet fruit that is said to heal one's voice.

Alignment: The snake plant, or *Sansevieria trifascia*, is dramatic with sturdy, tall, upward-growing leaves. Its bright, variegated color is soothing and makes a beautiful addition to a dull area of the home. Like a sword, its leaves cut through negative energy and embody precision and strength.

Harmony: Also known as the Swiss cheese plant (due to its large, bountiful, perforated, heart-shaped leaves), the *Monstera deliciosa* loves to climb. It grows quickly upward, inviting positive transformation.

the houseplant bagua mandala

Abundance:
African violet

Inspiration:
Oxalis triangularis

Nurture:
Orchid

Growth:
Pothos

Harmony:
Swiss cheese plant

Reflection:
Fiddle leaf fig

Insight:
Prayer plant

Wisdom:
Jade

Alignment:
Snake plant

a wild garden offering

Gardens of any size provide opportunities to offer intentional gifts to the nature spirits. Find a quiet spot for your offering, inside or outside, that is dedicated to the wisdom and wildness of the earth. The wild garden is a feng shui adjustment we learned from our teachers that we've adapted over time and now lovingly pass on to you.

Create space for your wild garden offering so it can flourish with only minimal and gentle human intervention. This offers the indigenous natural spirits of your home and land a place of their own. You can consider your wild garden offering, and the arrangement of objects within, as a miniature world.

1 Demarcate a circular space (inside or outside your home) for your offering. If it is indoors, use a wide pot or tray on a windowsill. Outside, you may opt for a circle created with stones or pebbles.

2 Include plants of any kind that will thrive in this location. The most auspicious numbers are three, five, or nine plants. Ask friends who have qualities you admire for plant cuttings or plant babies to include in your offering—the plants will be infused with their qi.

3 Set out offering bowls or cups in your wild garden. From time to time, you may leave gifts to share with the nature spirits. Gifts may include water, grain, alcohol (spirits), fresh flowers, or any other playful objects you wish to share.

Right You can create a wild garden offering with a round planter. There you can arrange a variety of plants and other elements of your choosing, including offering bowls or cups. The offering containers may also sit outside the planter.

your monthly qi forecast

- the 24 solar terms
- february: the cycle begins
- march: the seeds are planted
- april: spring peaks
- may: a time to bloom
- june: midsummer bliss
- july: big yang energy
- august: ground yourself
- september: productive and prepared
- october: reflection
- november: rest with gratitude
- december: meditative darkness
- january: time for self-care

the 24 solar terms

Above Our greatest feng shui teacher is nature. See what's happening outside, and even bring some of that qi into your home.

On the following pages, we offer a way to commence each month with a review of the energetic shifts that align with the cycles of the seasons and the natural world. Our intention is to inspire your curiosity, connection, and awareness, as well as to illustrate the subtle and profound ways that you are interconnected with your spaces.

Thousands of years ago, the ancient Chinese began to track seasonal shifts in their environment. They examined and identified changes in temperature, length of day and night, precipitation, flora and fauna, growth of crops, and so on. These observations were codified into 24 solar terms or micro-seasons to organize their planning around agriculture, as well as cultural and social events.

In exploring the Chinese calendar, it's helpful to acknowledge that these solar terms were developed in central China where the weather is more temperate than the drier, colder, northern part of the country. Geographic location impacts climate and seasonal shifts. For example, although they have the same latitude, the weather on a given day in New York City is probably not the same as in Naples, Italy. In addition, the calendar was created in the Northern Hemisphere, and follows the seasons there. Our friends in the Southern Hemisphere can adapt the monthly qi forecast for the six-month difference. For instance, in March, refer to the September qi forecast.

Regardless of where you are in the world, the dates and seasonal shifts vary and will often not be exactly aligned; however, the themes and teachings from the solar terms provide guidelines and generous gestural invitations to review your world. We encourage you to explore and find inspiration and guidance from the solar terms. Listen, look, receive, and be curious, and notice what is happening each month.

how to use your monthly qi forecast

Watching and observing the seasonal ebb and flow of nature illuminates and offers opportunities to deepen our understanding of feng shui philosophy. The changes in the seasons highlight the interplay of the five elements. In addition, the interaction between yin and yang is expressed by the long, dark, cold nights of winter (deeply yin) to the sunny, hot days at the height of summer (peak yang). Similarly, the cycles of the moon also teach us about yin and yang qi. When the new moon is dark in the sky, it is an opportunity for a yin offering of space, creativity, and manifestation. By contrast, the bright full moon is the fruition of yang qi and a time to let go and cut away. Each present moment is an invitation to live mindfully. We recognize and witness these concepts unfolding in nature, our best feng shui teacher.

home and heart

In this chapter, we offer a forecast describing the overall qi of each month. The descriptive names for the solar terms are often poetic and evocative, capturing the essence of that particular time of year, as are the names of the moon cycles. The elemental alignment explores the element of each month—for each one, we offer ways to integrate this qi into your home's feng shui with the home alignment, as well as ways to create a personal energetic connection with the heart alignment.

solar term and moon cycle dates

Each solar term lasts approximately two weeks, and the beginning of each one falls within the dates presented. The moon cycles shift annually. For exact dates, we recommend the Old Farmer's Almanac (see Further Reading, page 140).

Left Look to your lively green houseplants for the expression of spring's arrival. Check for new shoots and buds emerging, embodying the element of wood.

and flower buds are popping up all around. The energy is hopeful.

Constant Rain (February 18–20): Slushy rain falls as the days grow longer—it is damp, wet, and cold. The ice cracks, rivers and lakes begin to thaw. The water from melting snow seeps into the soil and becomes vital ground water, filling wells and cisterns essential for the drier months to come.

moon cycle

Historical names for the February full moon are "Snow Moon" or "Hunger Moon." With the energy of moon cycles in February comes a sense of something new: anticipation. Can you feel a stirring and the potential for a new beginning?

align with february's qi

Elemental alignment: What are the signs in your geographic area of water qi diminishing? Is the snow beginning to thaw? Where can you spot hints of wood element's arrival? For example, yin wood qi may be seen arising in the first flowers popping up amid patches of melting ice.

Home alignment: Hang a feng shui crystal in a window. The feng shui crystal ball is like a tiny sun in your home that channels pure white light, refracting it into rainbows. Set an intention to bring sunlight and warmth into your home and life.

Heart alignment: Visualize yourself cradling a ball of snow with both hands. Invite the warmth of the sun to thaw the ice, as a tiny plum blossom unfurls within it.

february: the cycle begins

The frozen earth will soon soften, and the snow is melting as the sun begins to strengthen. The month of February is the first solar term and marks the beginning of spring in the Chinese calendar. Nature anticipates the energy of wood stirring and moving upward beneath the soil. February, while still dark and wintery, offers the promise of brighter days with the yin energy of winter diminishing.

solar terms

Beginning of Spring (February 3–5): The first of the 24 solar terms. Depending on your geographic location and climate, there are varying signs of spring's arrival. For some the snow is just beginning to melt; for others new shoots

march: the seeds are planted

Rain showers help to thaw the soil. The cold chill is still present, but wood qi is strengthening, and in some areas, tulips are budding, forsythia is blooming, songbirds return, and robins pluck worms from the rain-soaked ground. It is time to clear the residue of winter.

solar terms

Awakening of Insects (March 5–7): Rain and thunder awaken the earth, and worms and small burrowing animals begin moving through the soft soil. The farmers can now harrow the fields, preparing them for planting.

Spring Equinox (March 19–21): This solar term celebrates when day and night are equal, after which the sun grows stronger and the days lengthen. For people in many cultures, it is a time to tidy their homes, inviting in the new energy of spring

moon cycle

The March full moon is known as "Worm Moon." The energy of the moon cycles in March is lively and active. You have woken up. Are you ready to break new ground? Be open to abundance and possibility.

align with march's qi

Elemental alignment: The colors associated with wood element are blue, green, and teal. Look for these colors in nature, like the green buds on a tree, or daffodils beginning to push up through the soil.

Home alignment: Clean your front door, the "mouth of qi," with the intention to bring new energy into the home. Let go of the dust and debris of winter with a spring clean (See Spring Equinox everyday magic ritual, page 116).

Heart alignment: Plant seeds or pot herbs for a new venture or project. Set your intention to cultivate new growth as you care for and nurture your little seedlings.

Right An active kitchen provides opportunities to clean year-round. Cleaning is especially auspicious in springtime when executed with intention.

april: spring peaks

The weather in April can vary tremendously. In some places, the cold and wet is now finally ending, while in others an explosion of wood energy is on full display. Trees burst into leaf and stunning cherry blossoms and magnolias provide a brilliant, if fleeting, show of color. Spring has settled in, and yang qi is now greater than yin.

solar terms

Clear and Bright (April 4–6): A promising time full of hope. Traditionally, in China, the first day of this solar term is also known as "Tomb Sweeping Day." It is a time to honor your ancestors by cleaning and tending to burial sites and the surrounding grounds.

Rain Showers (April 19–21): "April showers bring May flowers." This sounds quaint, but for farmers, reliable rainfall during this solar term is critical for the planting season. Newly seeded fields require regular intervals of rain to establish sprouts and new shoots. The weather in late April and early May can determine the outcome of the harvest many months away.

moon cycle

The full moon in April is rosy and optimistic. Its historical name, "Pink Moon" or "Sprouting Grass Moon," evokes images of fruit trees abundant with springtime buds. Align with wood energy of this full moon. What is sprouting or budding in your heart right now?

align with april's qi

Elemental alignment: During this wood season notice how you feel—energized and excited or maybe a bit rushed? Wood qi evokes fresh starts, active growth, and upward movement.

Home alignment: Discover which flowering trees are in season where you live—perhaps you can spot blooming pussy willow, dogwood, forsythia, or flowering almond. Procure some branches and arrange them on the dining room table or by the front door.

Heart alignment: Break in a new journal to collect your thoughts and plans. Which of the five elements align with the visions that you are ready to see blossom? Select a journal cover or an ink color to match and enhance this elemental energy.

Right The simple beauty of a single branch of spring blooms brings uplifted qi to any room in your home. Pair it with fresh water in your favorite vase.

may: a time to bloom

May is a celebration of fire qi and marks the official start of summer. The spring blooms have faded, farmers' fields are verdant with early crops, and foals and calves are born. May is a pleasant month filled with warm, sunny energy.

solar terms

Beginning of Summer (May 5-7): The commencement of summer is a joyful time for celebration. During this solar term you may experience the delight of fragrant blooms that make your heart sing such as lily-of-the-valley, wisteria, lilac, and honeysuckle.

Small Harvest (May 20-22): This term is an important agricultural time as spring crops grow taller, benefitting from the warmer temperatures. These longer, brighter days are full of active qi, with gardeners planting flower boxes and beds and farmers sowing their late summer and autumn crops.

moon cycle

The May full moon is known as "Flower Moon," and the moon cycles in May inspire you to unfurl and bloom. Imagine your own qi is like a fragrant flower, radiating joy.

align with may's qi

Elemental alignment: Observe the early signs of summer and notice how fire element manifests itself. For example, yin fire qi can be seen in the busy bees on bright red poppies.

Home alignment: Let your home breathe—open the windows and invite in the sun and fresh air.

Heart alignment: Sing out loud. Visualize your voice intermingling with your space and the qi beyond, carrying out into the world with your heart's song.

Left Notice the colors of May flowers that start to pop up in nature. Arrange them in bud vases around your home.

june: midsummer bliss

June displays the best of fire qi—warm, playful, and generous. As the sun sits high above us, yang qi is peaking, but the hottest days are still to come. These temperate June days bring vibrant trees, lush plants, and exuberant flowers.

solar terms

Sowing of Seed (June 5–7): This solar term is the last opportunity to plant seeds before the earth becomes too dry and hot. Warm summer rains shower the crops and encourage fruit to begin ripening. Bright red strawberries are picked and preserved. Hayfields are ready for their first cut.

Summer Solstice (June 20–22): The sun reaches its highest point and appears to stand still in the sky. Many cultures observe and celebrate this astronomical event with midsummer festivals. The longest day also marks the midpoint of the growing season, approximately halfway between planting and harvest.

moon cycle

June's full moon is known as "Strawberry Moon." As the sun shines a light on your gifts to the world, the moon reveals what might be hidden from you and what may need attention. Ask yourself: what is being brought to light?

align with june's qi

Elemental alignment: Fire element colors are red and fiery oranges. Bask in these colors where they appear in your world, like the stunning red leaves of a Japanese maple or sweet, red strawberries.

Home alignment: Notice the darkest and the brightest areas of your home. Notice the quietest and loudest areas. What are the most passive and the most active areas of your home? Attend to the areas that need uplifting.

Above Green foliage like a lush, leafy oak branch, or a tendril from a delicate plant like a fern, brings the verdant wood element into your home.

Heart alignment: Tune into the qi of fire. Wear a little red at your next social event to get noticed and meet new people. You are a beautiful soul! Don't be afraid to be seen. Also see the Summer Equinox everyday magic ritual, page 118.

Left Yin fire exhibits itself in the flame of a candle. Lanterns placed around your home and outdoor areas invite this gentle warmth.

Great Heat (July 22–24): This solar term is the height of summer. Many climates experience hot and humid conditions that peak with spectacular thunderstorms. Cool yin water, in the form of rain, is necessary to balance big, hot yang energy.

moon cycle

Bathe in yin qi during July's full and new moons for balance. The July full moon is known as "Buck Moon" or "Thunder Moon." If you are feeling burned out or overwhelmed, connect with this moon for peace and equanimity. What can be dissolved, and what can be brought to light?

align with july's qi

Elemental alignment: During this fire season, notice your emotions: do you feel bolder and more spontaneous or maybe a little too emotional? Fire qi is warm, generous, dynamic, and unpredictable. What has the sun brought to light?

Home alignment: Transform your bathroom into a restorative sanctuary with seasonal, fragrant flowers. Alternatively, mist the bathroom with an essential-oil flower blend, like rose or neroli.

Heart alignment: Soothe, cool, and hydrate your heart with water. Drink, swim, and bathe. Explore the color of water element with black crystals like shungite, black tourmaline, and onyx.

july: big yang energy

Typically, the hottest time of year, July has big yang energy. High temperatures and humidity conjure up dramatic thunderstorms. It's an active time with much fire qi swirling around. The world is illuminated and that which is hidden is revealed by the sun's brilliant light. You may find yourself seeking the cooling relief of yin water to balance the energy of this month.

solar terms

Minor Heat (July 6–8): This solar term describes the increase in temperatures and the fire element. Meandering fireflies display the subtle spark of yin fire. Fire qi inspires activity and visibility; being out in the world greeting new people and places feels natural at this time.

august: ground yourself

We treasure the last remaining days of summer. August is a time of transition. Take stock and establish roots as the big yang qi of summer recedes and the productive and fruitful activities of harvesting, picking, and cultivating commence.

solar terms

Beginning of Autumn (August 7–9): This solar term signals the shift toward autumn and is an in-between time of transition. Gradually the days begin to shorten, as energetic shifts are slow and incremental. For some locales, the hot, humid days linger, with autumn-like weather yet to come.

End of Heat (August 22–24): The hot summer begins to ease, with cooler mornings and refreshing evenings. Serene nights with dark, clear skies make for excellent stargazing. Many crops come to fruition at the end of August, which marks the start of the productive time for reaping and gathering.

moon cycle

Earth element embodies the boundary between seasons and encourages us to slow down. The August full moon is known as "Sturgeon Moon." It offers stability and grounding before the productive metal season marches in full swing. This is a time to be still and establish balance.

Right A bouquet of yellow flowers or a cheerful yellow chair can create a peaceful corner for self-care activities.

align with august's qi

Elemental alignment: Observe the hum of metal element emerging where you live. Yin metal qi can be seen in birds bravely and busily embarking on their migrations. What does the end of summer look like for you?

Home alignment: Stabilize the qi in your home with earthy and yellow tones. We love a bouquet of cheerful sunflowers in the bedroom.

Heart alignment: While standing in your bedroom, visualize yourself extending strong roots deep into the center of the Earth's core. Imagine drawing up the yellow light of earth qi through the soles of your feet to nourish your entire being.

september: productive and prepared

The harvest continues and farmers' markets are brimming with seasonal produce. September is abundant and bountiful. It is the first full month of the productive, metal-element season. The qi of this month urges us to complete unfinished projects, to gather supplies, and to begin preparations for the long winter ahead. Metal element supports us to minimize, reduce, and prepare to move inward.

solar terms

White Dew (September 7–9): The name of this solar term captures the qualities of qi present at this time. White is the color of metal element and water is the dew that clings to the woody grasses and cool earth. It evokes the bewitching charm of quiet mornings when the chill of yin energy has settled.

Autumn Equinox (September 22–24): The midway point of the autumn season. Many regions experience a dramatic temperature shift. The leaves on trees begin to change color. During this metal season, there are signs all around showing us that the natural world is preparing for the winter to come.

moon cycle

Let the dazzling September moonlight give you an extra boost. During the September full moon, known as "Harvest moon," set an intention to complete a lingering task or project.

align with september's qi

Elemental alignment: Notice how the metal element colors of gray, white, and metallics are displayed when you walk through nature. Observe pale gray in the sky, white within the bark of a birch tree, and silvery dew glistening on spider webs.

Home alignment: Schedule time to prepare for the winter by letting go of something in your home. It may be an ailing houseplant, a lamp in disrepair, or even those high-school jeans (see the Autumn equinox everyday magic ritual, page 120).

Heart alignment: Ring a metal bell or chime to invoke metal element when embarking on a project or autumn-decluttering session. Allow the sound to resonate all the way through your body and home, visualizing the vibrations cutting through any obstacles in your path.

Opposite Fruit represents completion and bounty, and reminds us to enjoy the sweetness in life.

october: reflection

October marks the continued transition of energy returning to the earth. Trees shed their leaves and plants die back; the qi is cool and contracting. The cycle of growth is coming to an end, inspiring a time to reflect and offer gratitude for the gifts and teachings of the year. As metal qi diminishes, the intuitive and mysterious energy of water emerges, making late October a thin, liminal time that facilitates connection with our ancestors and those we have lost.

solar terms

Cold Dew (October 8–9): Sweater weather officially arrives and bountiful post-harvest celebrations abound, embellished with gourds, pumpkins (and, of course, pumpkin spice!), hot apple cider, and pies. In the East, chrysanthemum tea is a traditional drink that warms and soothes.

Frost (October 23–24): Gardeners call this time of year the first "hard frost," when the dew freezes, icy crystals form, and sensitive plants and crops wither. Energy returns to the earth and will soon transition into cold, still water qi. Wood qi sleeps, vegetation dies, and nutrients return to the roots of perennials and trees.

moon cycle

The October full moon, known as "Hunter Moon," sparks wisdom-seeking, reflection, and intuition. What will you receive during this transition period? Be aware of insights that come to the surface during this potent time of self-discovery.

Opposite An easy way to connect with the calendar is to display seasonal flowers. Chrysanthemums and dahlias in deep ruddy tones invite autumn qi.

align with october's qi

Elemental alignment: How does metal element express itself for you at this time? When the trees let go of their leaves, they contribute to a system that nourishes the entire forest. When you let go of something, what are you creating space for that you wish to nuture?

Home alignment: Gather and arrange meaningful items in a special place in your home that you can visit from time to time. This can be an altar to connect with and offer sincere thanks to those who came before you.

Heart alignment: Sleep with a small mirror on your bedside table for nine days in a row. Each morning upon waking, gaze at your reflection and contemplate what arises from this exercise.

november: rest with gratitude

Icy, wintery, water qi arrives in November. The weather can be a mixed bag of cold rain, sleet, and icy puddles. The days become quieter, more restful, and shorter as we move into darkness. We carefully prepare and protect the precious grain stores, fields, livestock, and our homes from the impending winter and offer gratitude for the harvest that is safely tucked away.

solar terms

Beginning of Winter (November 7–8): An opportune time to warm your qi. Signs of early winter vary depending on the climate where you live. It may be a rainy season for some. For others, ice begins to form on lakes and ponds. Everything becomes a little slower and more restful. It is the start of the dormant water qi season.

Minor Snow (November 22–23): Temperatures drop significantly, and certain regions may see their first snowfall. It is essential to warm and nurture your qi. Bundle up in hats and scarves. Eat nourishing foods as the chilly winter season settles in.

moon cycle

The yin energy of the November moon asks us to welcome a slower pace. Historical names for the November full moon include "Beaver Moon" and "Frost Moon." Be inspired by nature as it shelters and hibernates, taking a much-needed rest. What in your life would benefit from a restful pause?

align with november's qi

Elemental alignment: Observe the early indications of water element where you live. What do you see in the outside world that makes you say, "Winter is coming"? Yin water qi exhibits itself in the frost that collects on fallen oak leaves.

Home alignment: Reignite the festivity of fire element in your home with lighting. Ambient light sources like small table lamps, twinkle lights, and candles can warm the dark corners.

Heart alignment: Soften, rest, and nurture your qi with fire element. On a small piece of paper, write down something that requires you to pause and reflect. Release and offer this paper to the flame of a candle with gratitude.

december: meditative darkness

Embrace the darkness of this solar term. Yin qi is dominant. In most locales, life hibernates beneath a thick billow of snow. It is frozen, still and black. Water element has a hidden and inward focus that offers restful and hushed serenity. This month is an opportunity to explore your unseen intuitive side.

solar terms

Great Snow (December 6–8): This solar term embodies the energy of fluffy snowflakes shimmering at night. At this time of year, we bow to the shortened daylight and extended dark nights as a part of nature's life cycle. We naturally sleep more, which strengthens our overall qi.

Winter Solstice (December 21–23): Yin energy peaks on the longest night of the year. Festive celebrations brighten and lift our bleak midwinter spirits. After the winter solstice, days will lengthen and yang qi will slowly gain more strength.

moon cycle

December's full moon is known as "Cold Moon" and "Long Night Moon." It teaches us to accept the darkness and the unknown while nurturing one's intuitive gifts. The moon + the longest night of the year = extra yin energy! What is your inner wisdom revealing at this deeply yin time of year?

align with december's qi

Elemental alignment: The colors associated with water are black and charcoal. Where can you see these colors in nature at this time? We can see water qi in the black velvety night sky, in the feathers of crows and ravens, and in the dark ice atop frozen ponds.

Home alignment: Festoon your entrance with red or fiery orange botanicals to invite the cheerful fire element to warm your home. Try branches of winterberry or red flowers like amaryllis. Also see the Winter Solstice everyday magic ritual, page 122.

Heart alignment: Sometime near the solstice and, ideally at noon, light a candle in the Inspiration area of your home or bedroom. After nine minutes, slowly move it to the Wisdom area with the intention to inspire luminosity and wisdom.

january: time for self-care

January is the chilliest month, when the ground is frozen and the weather is bitterly cold. We celebrate the turn of the new year (in the Gregorian calendar) as an opportunity to push the reset button, make resolutions, and set intentions. After weeks within deep, dark water qi, we may start to feel the winter blues, making January a perfect time for self-care.

solar terms

Minor Cold (January 5–7): The earth is hard, and may even be frozen solid in some climates. In rural areas, the amount of snow and frozen water in January can predict water levels in wells during spring and summer.

Great Cold (January 20–21): Earth qi settles in and buffers the seasonal shift between watery, still winter and lively, wood spring. Seasonal affective disorder can be common at this time of year. Connect with earth energy to nurture your body and spirit at this challenging time.

moon cycle

The energy of January's moon can feel barren and cold. After months of dark winter, we crave the warmth and glow of the sun. Practice self-care rituals for new beginnings during the new moon. During the full moon, offer aspirations for letting go. Historical names for the full moon are "Wolf Moon," "Ice Moon," and "Old Moon."

align with january's qi

Elemental alignment: In the depths of water season, consider journaling and contemplation. What offers self-care, nourishment, and creativity for you? What insights are revealed through the wisdom of sadness, solitude, and silence? Remember that water element connects us to our intuition.

Home alignment: Cultivate nurturing earth energy by hosting a cozy dinner party at your home. January can be a lonely month. Serve warm, spicy flavors to add a little fire qi to the gathering.

Heart alignment: Nurture and warm your qi with earth element. Imbibe hot, steamy drinks like apple cider, hot chocolate, and herbal teas. Don yellow or brown crystals like citrine, tiger's eye, and amber to bring the support of earth through color.

Right Warmth is essential to our health, especially in the colder months. A steaming mug of your favorite beverage stimulates all the senses.

mindful rituals for the seasons

- aligning with the seasons
- everyday magic ritual: mindful spring-cleaning
- everyday magic ritual: the magic of summer flowers
- everyday magic ritual: mindfully let go
- everyday magic ritual: alchemy of the hearth

aligning with the seasons

Above The magic of color is seen in our interior and exterior environments.

Over the course of a year, the Earth turns slowly as it orbits the sun, creating temperature and weather changes. As we learned in the previous chapter, winter is considered the most yin time because it is cold and dark, while summer is the most yang because it's bright and hot. Winter gently thaws into spring, spring warmly relaxes into summer, summer recedes lazily into autumn, and autumn cools into winter. Seasons move along at a thoughtful and slow pace, like an elephant, one step at a time. This creates a gradual, deliberate day-by-day shift.

We can begin to notice the nuances within each season and in their transitions by simply observing the world around us. A mindful walk in nature can teach us about how yin and yang present themselves in the seasons. For example, let's look at the yin and yang of the temperature in spring. Yin energy is still predominant in early spring when it's quite cold. Many climates even experience snowfall. In a few more weeks, we will see the spring equinox where the yang energy increases as the yin qi diminishes. It's a safe time to plant delicate crops or plants. More time passes as late spring eases into early summer, when the days get longer and warmer. By the time we have tipped into summer weather, yin and yang find a temporary equilibrium.

Each season is also connected to one of the five elements: wood, fire, metal, and water, with earth element easing the transition between each season. Spring is wood element, demonstrating growth and new beginnings. Summer is fire element: warm and exciting. Autumn is metal element; it's reflective and content. Winter is water element, being quiet and dormant.

embrace the cycles

Thoughtful acknowledgment of the seasons offers many teachings on mindful living. We can experience our interconnectedness with our world when we watch the seasons change in tandem with our human existence. When we are born, we burst at the seams with the youthful exuberance of spring, which eases into the full bloom that comes with mid-life. We feel the poignant longing that arises when we say goodbye to the warmth of the summer for the autumn of our later years. We taste our impermanence as we witness leaves wither and fall away. Finally, the winter comes when all is dark and our bodies disintegrate to rejoin the circle once again. This constant cycle of change is also observed within our daily schedule as well. We wake up to the spring of the morning light that brightens into high noon's apex. As the sun begins to set, we wind down our qi to finally rest into wintery sleep.

Within the seasons of continual change, a confidence and intrinsic stability arise when we witness these cycles year after year. We trust that the sun will rise every morning, which gives us security about our place in nature and how it connects to what is within our own hearts. We need not look far to find these profound teachings but simply open our eyes to the world we have inherited.

celebrating the seasons

All around the globe, annual ritual days remind us to align with our calendars, the season, and the environment. These ceremonies and holidays underline the importance of celebration in harmony with nature and our spaces, as our ancestors did generations before us.

On the following pages, we share an everyday magic ritual to honor each season. We drew from our personal practices, but we also encourage you to explore your own cultural and ancestral seasonal festivals and observances. These rituals may happen at any time. However, you can also celebrate each season on an auspicious day, like the solstice or equinox, with the intention of reconnecting to the fundamental seasonal qi at its peak.

These four everyday rituals are feng shui magic. Everyday mundane activities such as cleaning, appreciating a flower, decluttering, or simply cooking can become so much more with mindful intention and ceremony.

Above Modern life can distract us from basic human joys like skygazing under trees on a warm spring day, or simply noticing how a flower may close when the moon illuminates the night.

mindful spring-cleaning

Spring-cleaning can be a magical ritual when imbued with mindful awareness. There are numerous cultural practices that regard sweeping as a way to reset and start fresh. For instance, in a Japanese tea ceremony the host symbolically purifies utensils as part of the ritual to convey care and presence, as well as deep respect for the objects and the guests. In many Asian households, families prepare for the lunar new year by sweeping out the old to welcome in the qi of the imminent year.

We would like to emphasize that mindful cleaning is not about getting rid of the bad energy (or dust bunnies). Dust and difficult circumstances are gifts that guide us to notice what parts of our homes and lives need thoughtful attention. Therefore, we can also offer thanks to that which we are clearing away.

1 Open all windows and outside doors with the intention of inviting in fresh qi to cleanse and clear the space, objects, and structure of your home.

2 Sweep with intention to invigorate and move qi that has been dormant during winter. Start at the front door and move through the home as you finish up toward the back. If you have a back door, you can sweep any stale and stagnant qi out that way. Otherwise, use a trashcan to collect the qi that's ready to be released.

3 Mindfully clean your windows. Pay special attention to the areas you may usually neglect, like the sill and frames. Windows represent your eyes, perception, and clarity. Cleanse them with the intention of wiping away the debris that has accumulated over time, so that you can see things as they truly are, without obscuration and storylines.

4 Mindfully clean your doors. Doors are connected to the mouth and voice; they are how we interact with the outside world. Clean your doors so that you can receive qi, as well as polish your understanding and communication with others.

Right Bulb flowers like tulips and daffodils are early bloomers signaling spring's arrival. Honor the change of season with a bouquet of these cut flowers.

feng shui adjustments

While you mindfully clean, you are invited to include a few feng shui tweaks to enrich your ritual:

Meditation: Begin your spring-cleaning with meditation or simply a quiet, still moment. Close the ritual with gratitude to the dust bunnies for their teachings.

Mantra: You can sing or chant any mantra that is close to your heart while spring-cleaning your home. We enjoy the Buddhist mantra "Om Ma Ni Pad Me Hum" (the jewel is in the lotus).

Scent: Oranges and their scent invoke the yang qi of the sun, which will lift and brighten even the darkest of corners. An easy way to bring in this vibrant qi is to add 27 drops of orange essential oil to your non-toxic cleaning liquids.

the magic of summer flowers

Summer is an abundant, bright, and vibrant time when we see the Earth in full bloom, especially flowers. We love flowers — who doesn't? Flowers offer countless teachings. For example, cultivating or arranging flowers can teach us how to connect with nature. Flowers often accompany meaningful life events such as weddings or funerals, showing us how to appreciate beauty in the happiest and saddest of times. And most importantly, flowers remind us of our impermanence and that each fleeting human life is priceless and precious.

With so many flowers around, summer is a perfect opportunity to collect a flower essence and celebrate the energy of this season. A flower essence is the healing qi of the bloom that is gathered and programmed into water with mindful ritual and intention. Some ways to use the flower essence include adding nine drops to your drinking water, or creating a spray to mist around your aura or home. Create a flower essence with open curiosity about whatever teachings that flower has to offer you.

1 On a sunny summer day, calm your heart-mind with a few moments of silent meditation. Open your heart to welcome a flower to choose you. Then, explore a natural place with living flowers. This may include an indoor garden or some outdoor area.

2 Welcome a flower to choose you. When you meet your flower, request consent to participate in this ritual by asking her permission to create a flower essence. If you receive a no or a non-response, start again at step 1.

3 If you receive a yes to both requests, you may continue. Express sincere gratitude to the flower for its gift of participation.

Right We can appreciate and explore the qi of different flowers that we encounter. Look at the color and fragrance, and listen for any messages they want to share with you.

4 Gently place pure water (the best you can obtain) in a clear glass container close to the bloom. Leave it exposed to the full sun for a few hours. In addition, you may also use the light of the moon. If you are in a public place, even one hour is okay.

5 When you feel the flower essence is ready, strain off any debris, and collect the water into a clean colored glass bottle. Add 1 part water to 1 part brandy (or other high-proof liquor) or apple cider vinegar as a preservative.

6 Add nine drops of the flower essence to a bath (or foot bath) as soon as possible. While soaking in the bath, listen to what the flower wishes to share with you. Pay attention to the flower's biology, color, symbology, and more. Notice and receive any gifts, guidance, or insights from your new friend.

7 Label the bottle with the name of the flower and any other useful details like location, date, and so forth.

mindfully let go

Autumn trees begin to shed their leaves as the colors shift from verdant green to warmer yellows, browns, and reds. In the forest, the crisp leaves gather in piles, waiting patiently to decompose and nourish the Earth, as they continue to benefit the greater circle of life. Similarly, we invite you to notice how this may resonate with your relationship with clutter and letting go.

It is a common misconception that feng shui encourages reducing clutter. Rather, feng shui encourages us to notice and see how we may manifest and address challenges and obstacles, and how that may be expressed in our homes and lives. There's no requirement to become a "minimalist" to have good feng shui.

Instead, there is an invitation to appreciate and be present with the ebbs and flows of life, just like the autumn leaves that accumulate under the trees in the woods. If you do set up a declutter day in the fall, we recommend a mindful approach by noticing what is uncovered when you "rake" up the accumulation.

1 Sit in silent meditation somewhere inside your home.

2 Place both hands over your heart. Ask yourself for guidance in choosing one object to give away. Choose something of value and meaning for you.

3 Next, ask yourself to whom you can give this object. Allow this wisdom to arise from an intuitive, non-practical, yin space. Notice any feelings that arise. How do these thoughts connect to one of the five element styles (shown opposite)?

Left When letting go, be kind to yourself. Remember that it's also nourishing and supportive to be surrounded by the items you love.

4 If the item is too difficult for you to offer, start again at step 1. If it feel right to pass the object on, offer gratitude to the item and then give it away. Let it go, and don't look back.

your decluttering style

Autumn is connected to metal element. Its energy is like a fierce sword of compassion that cuts away what is no longer of service. So, naturally, this time of year also inspires decluttering as we start preparations for our winter hibernation.

The five elements offer insight and inspire curiosity to explore our experience of decluttering. Which one sounds most like you? Often you will embody and resonate with two, more, or even all of the element styles depending on the circumstances.

Wood: You start out with big plans and ideas, and much energy and enthusiasm, but quickly lose interest, leaving the project unfinished. Keep it short and sweet. Make letting go physical and actionable: you'll get a boost to meet your 10,000 daily step goal!

Fire: The things in your home make you feel happy, warm, and tingly in your heart. Much of your time is focused on revisiting memories and feeling the emotions of certain objects. You have permission to be as emotional as you need to be. Allow yourself space and time to touch in with your feelings.

Earth: You are a collector—your home is filled with many meaningful items and you have a hard time letting go of your possessions. It's okay to have things, but try to organize, take care of, and maintain your collections. Show them off by rotating what's on display, so your items are not

Above What parts of autumn mirror and offer opportunities for reflection on your own circumstances? We can trust in the greater wisdom of the Earth.

forgotten. Alternatively, consider how your practical and useful, yet dusty, collections may be offered to others. Your nurturing heart feels fulfillment when giving away what others can benefit from.

Metal: Decluttering is your middle name, and you may describe yourself as a minimalist. You keep your possessions under control and on a tight leash. Beware of over-purging—allow yourself to tap into your feelings a little more.

Water: It's difficult for you to let go of creative and wisdom-seeking items. You probably have stacks of books and artwork accumulating on the floor and you start reading your books as you try to pare down your collection. Lift your treasures off the ground. Place your books in bookcases and hang your art at eye level.

alchemy of the hearth

Across many cultures, the fire and the hearth are central to human comfort, health, and prosperity. In the modern age, the stove (or one's primary cooking appliance) is our modern hearth. It is a symbol of wealth and resources, and the central gathering place where fire element is harnessed and the family cooks meals, warms themselves, and prospers. And during the dark winter nights, the hearth illuminates and inspires hearts and minds, bringing the household together.

Another aspect of the hearth is the alchemy that happens when ingredients are assembled and transformed into a delicious healing meal that nourishes us. Within the womb of the receptive cauldron, we make offerings. The cauldron is open to receive what we give and, with fire, yields something new, imbued with our intention and magic. We each have the gift to transform and create change in the world.

Concoct a winter cauldron on your modern hearth (your stove or cooktop) and create alchemy using scent, botanicals, and the yang energy of oranges to warm, nurture, and shift the qi in your home. You can find an expanded audio-video version of this winter ritual at MindfulLivingBook.com (see Resources, page 140).

1 Gather a "cauldron" (a medium-sized pot will do), three oranges (or tangerines, clementines, or satsumas), spices, and botanicals. We love cinnamon sticks, bay leaves, cloves, star anise, and mint, but feel free to work with whatever you have in your kitchen cabinets.

2 Half-fill your cauldron with fresh water and place on the stove over a medium heat.

3 Cut each orange into nine slices, leaving the peel on. Place the orange slices in the cauldron.

4 Offer your choice of spices and botanicals to the cauldron.

5 Mindfully stir the mixture in a clockwise direction, whispering intention into the potion you've created. You can chant a mantra or even sing your wishes, intentions, and aspirations.

6 Allow the cauldron to reach a slow, steamy simmer. Reduce to the lowest heat setting before the water begins to boil.

7 Continue to simmer until the scent of the brew fills your home. Enjoy the cheerful and warming fragrance you have created with intention and visualize the magic as it permeates your space.

Above Make the winter cauldron your own creation. Play with scent and color, and choose spices and ingredients that resonate with you.

chapter 8

connections
to the natural
world

- nature symbols
- flowers
- fruit
- birds
- animals and mythical creatures
- earth and sky

nature symbols

Above We encourage you to be curious about symbols in your environment and to mindfully appreciate your connection to them.

Opposite Symbols offer opportunities for us to collaborate, innovate, and celebrate all living beings with sincere reverence and curiosity.

At its roots, feng shui is inspired by the connection of humans with the natural world. Much of feng shui is shamanic and animistic in its view of the universe. This means that there is a fundamental understanding within feng shui philosophy that everything is alive. This includes, but is not limited to, flora, fauna, stones, the oceans, and even the dust that accumulates in the quiet places in our homes. There's opportunity for balance, wisdom, and harmony to arise when we begin to acknowledge that we are all interconnected and interdependent on our little blue planet.

On the following pages, we've compiled a short list of symbols from the natural world and provided an example of how to explore each one in your home's feng shui. There are, of course, many, many more. We invite you to incorporate your own symbols and explore your own understanding and meaning for each one.

exploring nature symbols

Here are three simple ways to connect with nature symbols, both in your home and in your life.

Explore: Research, journal about, and contemplate what this symbol means to you.

Feng shui: Place the symbol in your home using feng shui principles. Examples include placement in a relevant room or bagua mandala area, or incorporating colors that embody the meaning in the display.

Integrate: Look for ways to include the symbol in your life. This includes wearing imagery of the symbol, creating artwork of the symbol, and so much more.

flowers

Flowers are symbols of beauty, abundance, and impermanence. In feng shui, freshly cut flowers invite life energy to flow smoothly through your space, as well as lift the mood of the household. Flowers invite joy and bring qi into otherwise dark spaces. While fresh flowers are ideal, you can also use flower imagery.

Chrysanthemum: This elegant flower is a sturdy and long-lasting autumnal bloom. As such, it is a symbol of resilience and longevity because it even thrives after the first frost. Arrange a bouquet of golden yellow chrysanthemums in the Harmony area of your home, or the center of any room, to support your health and well-being.

Lily: Lilies symbolize maternal and feminine energy. For instance, Western art and iconography use white lilies to represent Mary and, in China, orange and yellow day lilies are a symbol of a mother's love and compassion. Honor feminine energy and compassion with a bouquet of lilies in the Nurture area of your home or bedroom.

Lotus: The lotus is a symbol of rebirth and self-compassion. In Buddhism, it is a metaphor for our inherent, basic goodness, as it blooms with petals untainted from even the muddiest of water. In feng shui, lotus seedpods are also connected to fertility. Place an image of a lotus on your nightstand as a reminder to cultivate more compassion for yourself each day.

Left Offer a special seat or spot in your home for your symbolic flowers. A well-placed bunch of big, bold, golden sunflowers can uplift, and impart happiness and hope.

Orchid: In feng shui, the orchid symbolizes a charming, mature, and graceful romantic partner. If you care for it well, even when the blooms wither away, it will offer you beauty year after year. To invite a worthy, life-long romantic partner into your life, place an orchid plant in the Nurture area of your bedroom, or in a visible place such as the entryway.

Peony: The luscious peony is a symbol of prosperity and nobility and is connected to the abundance and verdant qi of spring. Place fresh peonies (or their image, when out of season) near the front door: red blooms for auspicious qi, pink for a gentle feminine touch, or purple to invite wealth.

Plum blossom: Branches of plum blossom are a symbol of winter, hope, and new beginnings. The first to bloom in late winter, plum blossom shows us that hope and beauty always exist. Display imagery of plum blossoms in challenging times, as a reminder to trust that spring is just around the corner.

Rose: Roses embrace the duality of soft, velvety petals amid sharp, thorny stems. They represent the complexities of a loving relationship and, in general, the need for compassion and understanding in difficult circumstances. Support your romantic partnership with fresh red roses in the bedroom, or pink roses if you're single and looking for a relationship.

Sunflower: Sunflowers are symbols of vitality, happiness, and the yang qi of the sun. They also represent fire energy, joy, and fulfillment. Place sunflowers, or their images, in the center or Inspiration area of your home to bring more vitality and cheer to the household.

fruit

Fruits are sweet gifts offered in abundance by the natural world. They symbolize harvest, wealth, and generosity. Even in modern times, Asian families often offer fruit at celebrations for auspicious prosperity all year round.

Apple: In Chinese, the word "apple" is a homonym for "peace." Apples represent the wish to share safety, wellness, and harmony. Place a bowl of red apples in your living room to welcome harmony and good friends into your home.

Calabash: The calabash is a fruit related to protection, long life, and healing. The dried, bottle-shaped gourds were used to store medicines in ancient China. The popular calabash shape is depicted in jewelry and vases, and it's easy to find the bottle gourds dried and decorated. Place one near your front door to provide protection for the home.

Grape: The ripe harvest of bountiful, purple and red grapes is synonymous with prosperity and celebration. In Tarot, grapes symbolize material wealth and abundance. Invite abundance into your household with imagery of grapes or vineyards in your kitchen or dining room.

Peach: Peaches are symbolic of youth, charm, and romance, and peach blossom represents luck (see chapter 2, page 35). In China they are also symbols of a long life; consider the legend of the Queen Mother of the West and her magical peaches that bestowed immortality on any who ate them. Depictions of peaches, or the color peach, can be used in the bedroom when in search of a romantic partner.

Pomegranate: The auspicious red color and abundant, vibrant, jewel-like seeds within the pomegranate lend this fruit its meaning as a symbol of fertility, legacy, and good fortune. For prosperity in offspring, be it with children or projects, add images or real pomegranates to the Reflection area of your bedroom or office.

Orange: One of the most important fruits in feng shui, the orange offers blessings and protection. Round and bright like a gold coin, oranges are auspicious symbols of good luck and positive, life-affirming qi. The fragrance, color, and imagery of oranges can be used in any room in your home that needs a qi boost.

Left Place a generous bowl of your chosen symbolic fruit in a meaningful room that complements your wishes and intentions. And be sure to partake of the bounty.

birds

In many cultures, birds are powerful, compelling symbols because they soar freely through the sky and communicate with the vast space of the heavens above. Their imagery embellishes palaces as well as the simplest of adornments, like jewelry.

Crane: Symbolizing long life, the graceful crane also grants wishes. It is said that if you fold one thousand origami cranes, your wish shall be fulfilled. Fold 9, 18, or 27 origami cranes and string them together with a red ribbon. Display them in a relevant area of the bagua mandala and make a wish!

Mandarin Ducks: As mates for life, a pair of mandarin ducks symbolizes marital harmony and fidelity. In some Asian traditions, wooden mandarin ducks are given as wedding gifts to promote a long and happy union. Place a pair of mandarin ducks, positioned so they are facing each other, anywhere in the home to reinforce devotion in a long-lasting and harmonious partnership.

Magpie: These highly intelligent, resourceful, and opportunistic birds are seen as symbolic messengers of joy and good news. Their black-and-white feathers are reminiscent of yin and yang energies. Enhance your strategic thinking and resourcefulness with imagery of magpies in the Wisdom or Insight area of your home or bedroom.

Above One way to display bird symbols is to place them slightly above eye level. This can offer the additional intention to invite more spacious freedom.

Left Bird imagery is well paired with fresh botanicals that bring in wood element.

Phoenix: A symbol of renewal, the mythical phoenix is also synonymous with purification and good fortune. For support and self-empowerment, add an image of a phoenix to the Inspiration area of your home or bedroom. This can be especially powerful if you're going through a difficult time.

Raven: Ravens are regarded as symbolic connectors of the seen and unseen realms. Their jet-black feathers, wisdom, and intelligence also nod to water element. If you encounter a raven while walking in nature, note what you are thinking about or doing at that moment. At home, explore the area of the bagua mandala that you feel is most connected to the message received.

Rooster: As a symbol of protection, the rooster's reliable crow banishes darkness and signals the arrival of dawn. In fact, it was customary in ancient China to release a rooster in a home before moving in to dismiss any unsavory qi. Place an image of a rooster near the front door as a sentinel to guard and protect the household. A rooster-themed weathervane placed on the roof will also suffice.

Songbird: Songbirds like sparrows, larks, cardinals, starlings, and robins lift the qi with their song and movement. These types of birds symbolize the thoughtful flow of qi that we can create through communication, intention, and action. Welcome songbirds into your garden with a bird feeder or even a birdbath and make sure it is maintained well.

Swan: Swans represent love and devotion and are cherished for their loyalty and dependability. Like mandarin ducks, they are said to mate for life. Place a pair of swans in the Nurture area of your home to invite a new partnership or support an existing one.

animals and mythical creatures

Many of us connect to animals as symbols of strength and wisdom. Look at the animals that resonate with you the most and see what messages they have to offer.

The 12 zodiac animals: The 12 animals of the Chinese zodiac are rat, ox, tiger, rabbit, dragon, snake, horse, ram, monkey, rooster, dog, and pig. Each one illustrates unique archetypal energies. Together, they offer true harmony, inclusive of all differences. Display a representation of all 12 zodiac animals in the order given above anywhere in your home to invite balance and harmony amid the variety of experiences and energies encountered within your life and household.

The 4 celestial animals: The four celestial animals, also known as the four emblems, include the red bird, green dragon, white tiger, and black tortoise. The four emblems often appear in a diamond formation and represent protection and ease. Grouped together, images of these four animals can be placed anywhere in your home as an expression of stability and support.

Butterfly: Butterflies are symbols of metamorphosis and change. In addition, pollinators like butterflies, moths, bees, and bats remind us to partake in the sweet nectar of life. Create a butterfly garden to attract these beauties to your backyard or use their likeness indoors to bring sweetness into your life.

Above This whimsical, butterfly-shaped mirror pulls sunlight into the room adding bright energy.

Cat: Cats represent the connection between the wild and domestic. In the Tarot, black cats are symbols of protection and an independent spirit. Real cats, or images of them in your home, can reconnect the wild and domestic aspects of you, as well as support your independence.

Dog: A symbol of loyalty and protection, the dog is also one of the 12 zodiac animals. Fu (or foo) dogs are mythical, lion-like sentinels found at the entrances to many Asian palaces, temples, and homes. Fu dogs come in pairs, the male with a ball and the female with a cub. Place them facing outward, guarding your front door. While standing in your doorway facing out, the male should be on the left and the female on the right.

Dragon: Representing benevolence, bravery, success, and good fortune, the mythical Asian dragon brings abundant rain and winds of change, with great success and prosperity. The dragon is also connected to earth element and the East direction, where the sun rises. In your home, place a dragon facing east to welcome new beginnings.

Sometimes you'll find a dragon holding a pearl (see opposite)—this is also known as "the wish-fulfilling jewel."

Elephant: Elephants are symbols of protection, majesty, power, and wisdom. The Hindu deity Ganesha is one of the most well-loved elephants and is known as the remover of obstacles. Place a representation of an elephant, like a statue, positioned to face outward at the main entrance of your home to invite wisdom and offer safety.

Fish: The gentle, constant movement of fish symbolizes a healthy flow of qi. The carp (goldfish or koi) represents great transformation and strength and is a reminder to receive challenges with bravery. An aquarium that is well cared for can invite positive energy and movement into your home, especially when placed in the living room or entryway.

Snake: Symbols of wisdom and intelligence, snakes are also a reminder to periodically shed your skin for new beginnings, transformation, or rebirth. An image of a snake in your bedroom or workspace can provide guidance during times of transition.

Turtle: Turtles and tortoises are connected to wisdom, longevity, and endurance. The ancient divinatory symbols that are the origin of the bagua mandala (see page 48) were said to be revealed on a tortoise shell. Consider including imagery of turtles in your home to enhance your health, harmony, and wisdom.

Left The color of a symbol enhances its feng shui meaning. How does the color of your symbolic object contribute to its intention?

earth and sky

Everything between heaven and Earth is part of us, including all the minerals and elements that make up our world. Together, we create the auspicious ecosystem that makes the magic of life happen.

Jade: This living stone is imbued with protective qi. It also represents strength and luck, and invites good health. Jade should be worn or displayed, not stored away or hidden in a drawer where it will become lifeless and brittle.

Lake: A symbol of joy, calm, peace, and contentment, a still lake also offers opportunities for reflection with its mirror-like surface. An image of a lake can be placed in the Reflection area of your home to help you cultivate more joy and contentment.

Moon: The moon embodies intuitive, yin qi and illuminates that which is hidden in darkness. On a full moon evening, open your windows and invite her light inside your home with the request to reveal and clarify.

Mountain: Mountains represent steadfast, observant wisdom. They are a symbol of perspective, meditation, and stillness. Enhance self-awareness and personal discovery with an image of a mountain placed behind the seat in your workspace, or in the Insight area of your home.

Pearl: Symbolically connected to intuition and the moon, pearls are also a metaphor for grace. Nurture the qualities of pearls by placing them on a home altar or on your nightstand.

Above A small bowl of sea salt can clear the qi of a room. You can also consider the symbols and colors on the bowl you chose for the given situation.

Pine: Evergreens survive harsh environmental conditions, and so the pine symbolizes integrity, dignity, and longevity. This tree also reminds us to respect our elders: our aged, weathered friends with stories to share. When in need of support, or in the face of adversity, the scent or imagery of pine will bring in the kindness and flexibility of wood element.

Salt: Salt is a crystalline mineral that absorbs and transmutes challenging energy and also a symbol of purity and rejuvenation. Place a small bowl or slab of salt in any room in your home to refresh the qi.

Sun: The sun represents bright, life-giving yang and active qi. In the Tarot, the Sun card symbolizes a positive and marvelous "yes!" as it's full of hope and promise. Open your windows and let in the sunlight. An especially auspicious time for this is between the hours of 11am and 1pm, local time.

living well with feng shui

- conclusion
- everyday magic ritual: creating your labyrinth

conclusion

Now we have reached our conclusion, we hope that you now have an understanding that there are many paths to living mindfully with feng shui. It's not just about rearranging the furniture or painting a door red, but rather about connecting to our hearts, our home, the land, and the world we've inherited as a whole. The many paths are what make feng shui a holistic practice. The everyday magic and energy of feng shui is truly the environmental art of living in mindful harmony with our spaces.

In the Introduction, we offered our own labyrinth story and invited you to walk alongside us through this book. Now it's time to carve your own journey, your own labyrinth. And so, we close with one final, everyday magic ritual with the reminder that each of us has the wisdom and insight to cultivate homes that heal our hearts. Thank you for walking the labyrinth with us.

OM MA NI PAD ME HUM:
The jewel is in the lotus.

creating your labyrinth

Draw a labyrinth to inspire contemplation and reflection. Our feng shui-inspired labyrinth begins with two simple lines: a vertical line crossed in the center by a horizontal line. The first line, conceptually up and down, connects heaven and Earth. Then the second line, drawn across the center of the first, from one side to the other, symbolizes the directions east and west. Next are four dots, as if creating the corners of an invisible square around the cross. Finally, the eight directions represented by the lines and dots are joined together by a series of concentric lines, letting the life-force energy flow and the labyrinth come to life.

To begin, we recommend you use a finger to energetically trace the labyrinth in this book with the intention of receiving the everyday magic of feng shui teachings into your life. Once you get the hang of it, you can practice this with paper and pencil. You can also trace an invisible labyrinth on objects in your home, like a bed, stove, or desktop.

In addition, these instructions include dialogue (shown in italics) that you can recite. These words may be vocalized out loud or whispered quietly within your heart. For an audio-video version of this guided meditation, see Resources (page 140).

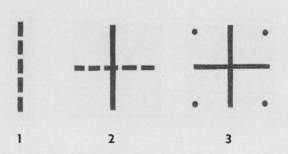

1 Draw a vertical line, from bottom to top, and chant:

"As above, so below. We call in the elements of black water from the north, and red fire from the south."

2 Draw a horizontal line from left to right, crossing the first line through the center, and chant:

"Connecting yin and yang. We call in the elements of green wood from the east, and white metal from the west."

3 Draw four dots in each of the invisible four corners around the cross: bottom left, top right, bottom right, and top left, and chant:

"From the northeast, we call in the mountain. From the southwest, we call in Mother Earth. From the northwest, we call in Father Sky. And from the southeast, we call in the wind."

4 Bring your labyrinth to life by connecting the lines and points with smooth curved lines, as shown right, creating the path for qi to flow. Chant:

"We open our hearts to receive the flow of everyday magic from all eight directions."

5 To close the ritual, place both hands over your heart center and chant:

"With tremendous gratitude and sincerity, we offer this gift to all sentient beings, including ourselves."

4a 4b 4c 4d

resources

Study directly with Anjie and Laura
at Mindful Design Feng Shui School:
https://mindfuldesignschool.com

The Holistic Spaces website offers an online
shop where feng shui related items can be
purchased, including feng shui crystal balls:
https://holisticspaces.com

Listen to the Holistic Spaces Podcast here:
https://holisticspaces.com/podcast

Follow us:
Instagram @mindfuldesignschool

Learn more about Laura Morris:
https://morrisfengshui.com

Learn more about Anjie Cho:
https://anjiecho.com
Instagram @anjiecho

For expanded audio-video versions of the rituals
and meditations featured in this book, visit
MindfulLivingBook.com, or scan the QR code:

further reading

Huang, Alfred, *The Complete I Ching*
(Inner Traditions International, 2010)

Thomas, Robert B., *The Old Farmer's Almanac*
(Old Farmer's Almanac, 2023)

Wing, R.L., *The I Ching Workbook*
(Bantam Doubleday Dell Publishing Group, 1978)

Wilhelm, Richard, and Baynes, Cary F.,
The I Ching or Book of Changes
(Princeton University Press, 1979)

index

Page numbers in **bold**
indicate an illustration

abundance *xun* 52,
    62, 90
African violet 90, **91**
alignment *qian* 55,
    64–5, 90
altars 109
amber 111
amethyst 37
ancestors 100
animals 133–4
animism 126
apples 130
attentiveness 14
aubergine (color) 37

back doors 76–8
bagua mandala *see also*
    floor plans
    abundance *xun* 52, 62
    alignment *qian* 55,
        64–5
    bedroom 58–9
    card spread ritual 56–7
    divination 44–6
    exploration 60–5
    growth *zhen* 51–2, 62
    harmony *tai qi* 55, 65
    I Ching 46
    insight *gen* 51, 61
    inspiration *li* 52, 63
    nurture *kun* 52, 63
    overview of design
        48–9
    reflection *dui* 55, 64
    wisdom *kan* 51, 61
balance 32
balconies 83
bathroom
    in alignment *qian* 83
    exploration 25

in harmony *tai qi* 75
in insight *gen* 85
monthly forecast 104
bedroom 26, 58–9, 105
beds 26, 82
bells 64, 71, 76, 106
birds 131, 133
black 31, 38, 104, 110
blackberry (color) 37
blue 25, 31, 36, 61, 99
books **23**, 61
bracelets 40
breath/breathing 18, 65
brown 37
BTB (Black Sect Tantric
    Buddhist) lineage 9
butterflies 133

calabash 130
candles 63, 110
cars 76
cats 133–4
cauldrons 122–3
center 55
chairs 22, 27
chalk 38
charcoal 31, 38, 110
chrysanthemum 129
cinnabar 34
circles 40
citrine 111
citrus fruit 25, 35
cleaning 60, 99, 100,
    116–17
clutter 120–1
coins 62
color *see also individual*
    colors
    bagua mandala 60
    bathrooms 25
    color circle ritual 40
    dining room **22**
    elements 31, 74

exploring 30
individual experience
    33
missing areas 72
pigments 33
qi 33
commanding position
    26, 80–3
crane 131
cream 38
crystals 27, 63, 65, 98,
    104, 111

daily cycle 115
decluttering 120–1
desks 26, 82, 84
dining room 22
divination 19, 44
dogs 134
door mats 21, 71
doors 21, 76–9, 99, 116
dragons 133, 134
dragon's blood 34
ducks 131
dust 20, 60, 99, 116, 126

earth 31, 111, 121, 135
earth tones 31, 105
eggplant (color) 37
elements 31, 74
elephants 134
energy *see* qi
entry foyer 21
extensions 73–5

feng shui
    overview 14
    translation of term 18
feng shui schools 9
fiddle leaf fig 90, **91**
fire
    color 31
    kitchen 25

monthly forecast 102,
    103, 104, 110
personality 121
seasonal changes 114
fireplaces 75
fish 134
floor plans
    bagua mandala
        overview 68–9
    commanding position
        80–3
    extensions 73–5, 84
    garages and secondary
        doors 76–9
    missing areas 70–2,
        84, 85
    small homes 84–5
flow 18
flowers
    bathrooms **25**
    color **10**, 30
    dining room 22
    elements **32**
    flower essences 118–19
    inspiration **15**
    monthly forecast 102
    seasonal changes **117**
    symbols and meaning
        129
    variety **11**
focal points 22
food storage 25
front door 21
fruit 25, 62, 130
fu dogs 134
fuchsia 34

Ganesha 134
garages 76, 78
gardens 92
gold 38
grapes 130
gratitude 110, 121

gray 31, 38, 106
green 25, 31, 36, 99
growth *zhen* 51–2, 62, 90
gua 46, 48–55

harmony *tai qi* 55, 65, 90
heart alignment *see* monthly forecast
hearths 122–3
home *see also* floor plans
as energy source 16
qi 69
as reflection of self and life 47

I Ching 46
indigo 36
insight *gen* 51, 61, 90
inspiration *li* 52, 63, 90
iron blue 36

jade stone 135
jade succulent 90, **91**
Japanese tea ceremony 116
journals 61, 100, 111

kitchen 25, 78

labyrinths 8, 10, 138–9
lakes 135
lapis lazuli 36
lavender (color) **33**, 37
lifecycle 115
lighting 21, 63
lily 129
limestone 38
living room 22
lotus 129

magic 6–7, 14, 88
magpies 131
mandala 45 *see also* bagua mandala

mandarin ducks 131
mantras 117
meditation 61, 90, 110, 117, 120
metal 31, 105, 106, 109, 114, 121
mirrors
bathroom 75
bedroom 26
desks 84
missing areas 72, 85
monthly forecast 109
reflection *dui* 64
wisdom *kan* 61
monstera 90, **91**
monthly forecast
April 100
August 105
December 110
February 98
January 111
July 104
June 103
March 99
May 102
November 109–10
October 109
seasonal changes 96
September 106
solar terms 96–7
moon 135
moon cycles *see* monthly forecast
mountains 51, 61, 135
movement *see* flow

nature symbols 126–35
numbers 25, 40, 62
nurture *kun* 52, 63, 90

obsidian 27, 38
ochre 35
onyx 38, 104
oracle cards 56–7
orange (color) 31, 35, **44**, 103, 110

oranges (fruit) 25, 117, 122, 130
orchid 90, 91, 129
origami 131
Oxalis triangularis 90, **91**

peach 35, 130
pearls 135
peony 129
phoenix 131–2
pigments 33
pine trees 135
pink **22**, 34
plants *see also* flowers
bagua mandala 89
bathrooms 25
caring for 89
growth *zhen* 62
magic 88
missing areas 71, 72, 85
nurture *kun* 63
seeds 90, 103
shifting qi 90
workspace **27**
plum blossom 129
plumbing 25
pomegranate 130
pothos 90, **91**
prayer plants 90, **91**
Prussian blue 36
purple 37

qi *see also* monthly forecast
bagua mandala 60
color 33
definition 14
dining room 22
elements 31
entry foyer 21
in the home 19
overview 18
shifting with plants 90

ravens 132
red **10**, 30, 31, 34, 103, 110
reflection *dui* 55, 64, 90
rhodonite 63
rituals
alchemy of the hearth 122–3
bagua mandala card spread 56–7
color circle for healing 40
flower essences 118–19
labyrinths 138–9
letting go 120–1
room-by-room exploration 20–7
spring cleaning 116–17
usage 10
wild garden offering 92, **93**
room-by-room exploration ritual 20–7
roosters 132
rose 129
rose quartz 34, 63
rugs 26

salt 135
seasons 114–23 *see also* monthly forecast
seating 22, 27
shamanism 126
shapes, bagua mandala 60–1
shell pink 34
shrines 109
shungite 27, 104
silver 38
singing 102
snake plant 90, **91**
snakes 134
solar terms 96–7
songbirds 132
spring cleaning 90, 116–17

storage 25
stoves 25, 78, 82, 122–3
sunflower 35, 105, 129
sunflowers 135
swans 132
symbolism 45–6

tangerine 35
Tarot 56–7, 129, 133–4, 135
teal 25, 31, 36, 99
thunder 51–2
tigers 133
tiger's eye 111
toilets 25
tortoises 133, 134
tourmaline 27, 104
trees 62, 71, 100, 106, 109, 135

trigrams 46, 49
turtles 134

umber 37

vermillion 34
violet 37
visualization 61, 64

walking 62, 114
water
    bathrooms 25
    color 31
    kitchen 25
    monthly forecast 98, 104, 109–10
    personality 121
    qi 18
    seasonal changes 114
    wisdom kan 51, 61, 90

white 31, 38, 106
wind 18, 52
wind chimes 64, 71
windows 102, 116, 135
wisdom kan 51, 61, 90
wood
    color 31
    monthly forecast 98, 99, 100
    personality 121
    seasonal changes 114
workspace 25–6

yang
    living room 22
    monthly forecast 104
    overview 16–17
    seasonal changes 96, 114

yellow 10, 31, 35, 54, 65, 105
"yes/and" paradox 16–17
yin
    monthly forecast 110
    overview 16–17
    seasonal changes 96, 114

zinc oxide 38
zodiac animals 49, 133

picture credits

All photography and illustration © Ryland Peters and Small/CICO Books except as otherwise listed below.
t=top, l=left, c=center, r=right, b=bottom

Floor plans on pages 59, 69t, 71, 75, 79, 83, 85 © **Anjie Cho**
Simon Brown: pages 1, 10, 18, 23, 24, 30, 31 (earth), 36bc, 39r, 65r, 70; **Rachel Whiting:** pages 2, 11, 12, 15, 31 (wood), 35bc, 36t, 36bl, 38bc, 42, 48, 62, 72, 76, 78, 84, 86, 88, 91c, 98, 99, 103, 108, 114; **Emma Mitchell:** pages 3, 26, 35bl, 37t, 37bc, 47, 50, 61, 66, 82, 89, 94, 112, 124, 132; **Debbie Patterson:** page 4; **James Merrell:** pages 7, 96; **Debi Treloar:** pages 9, 19, 22, 28, 34bc, 36br, 37br, 39l, 41, 53, 54, 63, 64, 81, 101, 105, 115, 120, 121; **Jonathan Gregson:** pages 16, 111; **Maulana (Vecteezy):** pages 17, 49, 55, 65l; **Polly Wreford:** pages 21t, 38bl, 73; **Jan Baldwin:** pages 21b, 77, 133; **Catherine Gratwicke:** pages 25, 34br, 35br, 38br, 58, 134; © **artjafara (Adobe Stock):** page 27; **Ian Wallace:** page 31 (fire); **Peter Cassidy:** pages 31 (metal), 130; **Barco Clara (Getty Images):** page 31 (water); **William Reavell:** pages 32, 35t, 44, 69b, 131; **Kim Lightbody:** page 33; **Caroline Arber:** page 34t; **Claire Richardson:** pages 34bl, 117; **Gavin Kingcome:** pages 35bl; **Mark Lohman:** pages 37bl, 128; **James Gardiner:** pages 37bc, 82, 124, 126, 132; **Joanna Henderson:** page 38t; **Maciej Wojtkowiak (artdirectors.co.uk):** page 45; **Melissa Launay (*The Golden Tarot* by Liz Dean):** page 57; **Helen Cathcart:** pages 74, 91tr, 91bl, 93, 102; **Penny Wincer:** pages 80, 127; © **Sunny_Smile (Adobe Stock):** page 91tl; © **Kulbir (Adobe Stock):** page 91tc; © **Maritxu22 (Adobe Stock):** page 91cl; © **Olga Miltsova (Adobe Stock):** page 91bc; © **julijadmi (Adobe Stock):** page 91br; **David Brittain:** page 104; **Erin Kunkel:** page 107; **Melanie Eclare:** pages 119, 138; **Jo Tyler:** page 123; **Dan Duchars:** page 135; © **nono (Adobe Stock):** page 136; **Victoria Fomina:** page 139

acknowledgments

We offer our sincerest gratitude to our feng shui mentors. A special thanks to Katherine Metz for writing the foreword and diligently reviewing our manuscript. In addition, we acknowledge our deepest appreciation for our teachers' teacher: His Holiness Grandmaster Professor Lin Yun. We would also like to thank our Mindful Design School students, some of our greatest teachers.

From Laura: Thank you to my mother, my first and best teacher. And to all my Tarot, yoga teachers, and soul guides past and present, especially Jayne Marie and Stephanie Mills. Thank you to my beautiful family. I love you all. And most importantly, to my love, Stuart, and to my amazing son, Declan.

From Anjie: Finishing up my third(!) book, I'm so grateful for the love, support, and kindness from my family, especially Jeremiah, Javier, and Pearl. Thank you to all my followers for reading my books and allowing space for my voice to be heard.

This book would not have been possible without the support and persistence of our literary agent William Clark, as well as our editors at CICO, Kristine Pidkameny and Carmel Edmonds.